ON
CLOWNS

*The Dictator
and the Artist*

ALSO BY NORMAN MANEA

October, Eight O'Clock

ON
CLOWNS

The Dictator and the Artist

ESSAYS BY

NORMAN MANEA

GROVE WEIDENFELD

New York

Collection copyright © 1992 by Norman Manea
"Romania: Three Lines with Commentary" translation copyright © 1990 by Norman Manea
"On Clowns: The Dictator and the Artist," "Felix Culpa," "The History of an Interview"
translations copyright © 1992 by Grove Press, Inc.
"Censor's Report" translation copyright © 1990 by Northwestern University Press

Published by Grove Weidenfeld
A division of Grove Press, Inc.
841 Broadway
New York, NY 10003-4793

Published in Canada by General Publishing Company, Ltd.

The publisher is grateful for permission to reprint the following:
"Romania: Three Lines with Commentary" from *Without Force or Lies,* published by
Mercury House, San Francisco, 1990. Reprinted by permission.
"A Poet" by Eugenio Montale from *It Depends,* copyright © 1977 by Arnoldo Mondadori
Editore Sp.A. Translated by G. Sinkh. Reprinted by permission of New Directions
Publishing Corporation.
"The Censor's Report" from *Formations,* vol. 5, no. 3, Winter–Spring 1990. Used by
permission of the publisher.
"Felix Culpa" first appeared in a different form in *The New Republic.*

Library of Congress Cataloging-in-Publication Data
Manea, Norman.
On clowns: the dictator and the artist / Norman Manea.—1st ed.
p.   cm.
Translation.
ISBN 0-8021-1415-6 (alk. paper)
1. Manea, Norman. 2. Literature and society—Romania.
3. Socialism and literature—Romania. 4. Romania—Politics and
government—1944– . 5. Authorship. 6. Censorship—Romania.
I. Title.
PN51.M265   1992
949.8—dc20   91-23866
                                                    CIP

Manufactured in the United States of America
Printed on acid-free paper
Designed by Irving Perkins Associates, Inc.

First Edition 1992

1 3 5 7 9 10 8 6 4 2

"I am nothing but an Irish clown," he said, "a great joker at the universe."
—JACQUES MERCANTON, *The Hours of James Joyce*

CONTENTS

AUTHOR'S NOTE

Upon my arrival in the West a few years ago, the urge to describe what my life had been like under the dictatorship in Romania—and more important, what I had learned from my experiences—clashed with a reluctance to add to the exposés of suffering already classified and commercialized in the repertory of East European dissidence.

No matter how phantasmagoric its stagings often were, the totalitarian society from which I had come was not, as Western audiences prefer to believe, some sort of unearthly, demonic aberration, but a human reality that still persists and may indeed revive in other guises as an ideology and as a form of society.

At the onset of my exile, I wished to discuss the relationship between the writer, the Power, and the not-so-innocent oppressed masses. And the relationship between the writer and his own vulnerability, of course.

In any political system that uses culture as a weapon (by honoring the artist with exaggerated privileges or penalties), the writer continually faces traps meant to compromise and gradually destroy his integrity, and thus his identity. He has to learn to defend himself, especially from mental traps, from simplistic visions, not only inside totalitarian systems, but everywhere. What seem to be elementary polarities often prove to be in fact complementary. As is well known, many antifascists were Communists; often enough, adversaries of one totalitarian system (fascism, communism, religious fundamentalism) are, consciously or unconsciously, advocates of another. But the authentically liberal spirit of democracy is not only opposed to totalitarianism; it is alien to it, and is by its very nature above polarities.

In a lifelong attempt to avoid these kinds of traps, I have developed a firm skepticism toward political kitsch and a constant suspicion of its manipulatory labels. Even after the Communist mask has fallen from the tired, disfigured faces of the millions of captives in Eastern Europe, now plunged in the painful and prolonged transition toward civil society, my skepticism and suspicion have not diminished. Yet on the other shore, a self-congratulatory society took the collapse of the *other* side as a vindication, all the while avoiding a sharp look at itself. As an outsider to both systems, I couldn't fail to notice the double irony.

Many questions arose in my first years as an exile, in the complicated transition from one shore to the other. Adapting to a new world is not unlike somersaulting into the void. The shock is not only linguistic. It is not hard to imagine why there is usually a delay before an exile can resume writing, and why writing in exile continues haltingly. So far I have been able to address only a few of the subjects that have preoccupied me.

The present disparate essays—for better or worse subject to a certain journalistic, rhetorical dialectic—are all obsessed with the relationship between the writer and the totalitarian ideology and society in a country whose political tradition was never admirable and where the dictatorship of the last several decades was a picturesque mixture of brutality and farce, of opportunism and demagogy. One can understand why the guilt of those who allowed themselves to be duped by totalitarian utopias, whether of the right or left, was not a *felix culpa* as Mircea Eliade thought, and why the merry masks of those rewarded for their daily complicity with the Power have provoked not only laughter.

But for many, life in captivity meant resistance, solidarity, and all the suffering and hope that they entail. The wounds, however, are lasting. They've left this convalescent with no more than a moderate optimism, no matter on which meridian his future is taking new roots. Perhaps that is why the vivacity of victory and the joy of liberation do not abound in these pages.

In 1945, a child returning from the concentration camp, I was given a book of folktales. I still remember this first gift, its thick, green covers, the magic of that encounter: the word as miracle. Only later, and perhaps inevitably, was I obliged to discover that the word is also a weapon against or in defense of humanity.

While writing these essays I have had—as in former times when I was writing other books, especially *Auguste the Fool's Apprenticeship Years*—plenty of occasions to think about the process of formation through deformation, about the conflict between individual aspirations and the oppressive, stifling pressure of the "great beast," as Simone Weil called society. In a totalitarian state, the closing off of society and the impressment of individuals into an amorphous mass became a total prison made up of private and state-owned cages guarded not only by wardens but by fellow citizens: a brutal solution to societal conflicts that democracies confront humanely and even efficiently.

I can imagine the social apprenticeship of any individual anywhere as the adventures of an Auguste the Fool misled by deceptive promises. All the more so the life of the artist, a professional creator of chimeras.

Nevertheless, the totalitarian experience is incomparable, an extreme situation whose limits can always be extended, whose potential for evil gives rise to a cancerous social pathology. This society is not monolithic, as the Communists hoped and many anti-Communists maintained; instead it was characterized by ambiguity and duplicity, masks and falsehoods. Only the circus master and his animal tamers believed in the absolute magic of terror and the mesmerizing effects of false rewards. If the totalitarian tragedy is not to be forgotten, then neither is the totalitarian comedy—they are inseparable. The writer, an extreme element in that extreme situation, became a symbol for the impasse of the entire society.

If he is to remain honest, the survivor cannot allow himself frivolous illusions or exaggerated laments. As a writer, this survivor can best understand, paradoxically, that the game of art will always confront but never tame the "great beast." The fact that Gustave Flaubert saw himself as a *saltimbanque* does not seem an affectation: the ironic revenge the writer can have is to parody, in his fiction, the Great Adversary himself.

Bard College
June 1991
Translated by Cornelia Golna

ON
CLOWNS

The Dictator
and the Artist

ROMANIA

THREE LINES
WITH COMMENTARY

". . . the demon of sadism and stubborn stupidity."

"If only our administration and politics were on the same level as the arts . . ."

". . . a country inhabited by people and books."

I

"In Legionnaire, bourgeois, nationalist Romania I saw the demon of sadism and stubborn stupidity incarnate before me." Although Eugène Ionesco wrote these words in 1946, he did not elaborate on them until many years later, in the volume *Présent Passé, Passé Présent* (Paris, 1968).

That sentence has haunted me in recent years. Especially the question of how many words—and which words—would have to be changed in order for the statement to apply to our current situation.

As a child I lived through the ordeal of hatred and war in Legionnaire,[1] bourgeois, nationalist Romania. Later I looked at

---

[1] "Legionnaire" refers to Romanian Fascist organizations like the Legion of the Archangel Michael, later the Iron Guard.

3

many books, documents, literary and artistic representations, all sorts of studies, to try to comprehend the Nazi phenomenon not only in its German but also in its other European varieties, and to find an explanation for these terrible derailments of history, of society, of the psyche (which is to say, of humanity itself); an explanation for the bewilderment and despair of constantly larger strata of the population; an explanation for the gradual extinction—through terror—of civil society and the transformation of everyday life into a state of siege in which the external "enemy" becomes a pretext for the extermination of "suspects" inside the citadel.

But only in the last years did I begin to understand the mechanism that sets off such inexorable disasters. Romania, under the most cruel and dark dictatorship, pressed by a deepening economic, political, and moral erosion, presented me with the very model of a collapse in which, this time, I did not play the part of a guinea pig—as I did in my childhood—but of an observer, and even of a not yet completely disarmed "suspect."

More than once I was reminded of Bergman's film *The Serpent's Egg*, of the stultifying atmosphere of the last years of the Weimar Republic, of the mixture of paranoia and disorientation, of the ways in which discouragement turns into resignation, then submission, and how general dissatisfaction hurries to find marginal targets; of how, given conditions of unalleviated material want and systematic terror, stupidity and violence will erupt wherever they can.

Still, let me hasten to say that—despite quite a few similarities— the Romania of the 1980s was not the Legionnaire, bourgeois, nationalist Romania of the prewar and wartime period.

The recent controversies in the West over the similarities between nazism and communism overlook, perhaps not entirely innocently, the much more important differences between the two systems. This cliché stems from the comforting simplification that to demonstrate the equally catastrophic effect of all dictatorships is to hold them all equally culpable; but this would lead to a relativization of guilt, and therefore, ultimately, to exoneration.

Not even the way that the two systems sometimes "borrow" methods from each other makes them equivalent. Those who want to understand something essential about "real socialism" (but also those interested in the character and consequences of national socialism) should begin by studying the important differences between nazism and communism. Communism espouses a generous and widely accepted humanitarian ideal and utilizes subtler, more duplicitous strategies, which may at least partly explain its respectable age and incomparable expansionist force. Nazism was, in all its deeds and misdeeds, consistent with its own program, and those who followed it, at least in the initial stages, embraced that program knowingly and "legally." On the other hand, communism is, in the balance sheet of relations between utopian vision and reality, in sharp contradiction with itself, and imposes its system on the masses by force. A contradiction between ideology and the concrete necessities of government, between the posited ideal and the reality that challenges it—but, paradoxically, this contradiction also offers the Communists their relative capacity for recovery, for regeneration, and of course also for mystification. And it is in this ample field of inconsistencies and incongruities that demagogy operates and society manifests its elasticity; it is here that vital processes— the movements of ordinary daily existence—act.

Comparisons between the two systems, however, are not uninteresting, nor are their similarities insignificant. The unlit streets of Bucharest, the unheated apartments, the interminable lines for basic foodstuffs, the ubiquity of the police and its collaborators, the diversionary attacks on national minorities, the increasing brutality in human relationships, the monstrous pressure exerted by the bureaucracy in every sphere of material and spiritual life—all this reminded me again and again of Bergman's film about the years before Hitler's seizure of power, of that stifled atmosphere, that confused immobility perpetually poised between implosion and explosion. Life as a series of postponements, a tumorlike growth of mistrust and fear, an all-encompassing schizophrenia. A step-by-step reduction of private life, and finally its abolition, as time itself becomes subject to ever-increasing taxation and eventually total *expropriation* by the state: the hours sacrificed to standing in lines, to ritual political meetings and to rallies, on top of the hours at work and the hours of helpless exposure to the inferno of public transportation on the way to and from work, meetings, and shopping; and when you were finally home in your birdcage, you found yourself lost, mute, staring into an emptiness that could be defined as infinite despair.

The vacant stare, the mind in a void, tortured by the question of whether the evil embodied in its one face (one computer portrait of evil in hundreds of printouts) was due to an unfortunate accident, a derangement of history itself, and therefore not to an individual psychological disturbance; or whether it was something latent in all people at all times that had now erupted as this monstrous collective fate.

Everywhere there was the insidious, dilated presence of the monster called the Power. In one's home, in one's thoughts, in the conjugal bed. The power of darkness. The black hole haunted by the demon of sadism and sly, stubborn stupidity. Tirelessly active impersonality, self-affirmed by a huge cult of the dictator's personality, proving itself and confirming its power by suppression. The void that knows no barrier. The polarization of malignant energy. *He, she:* "the others." Nepotism as an instrument of tyranny. The festivities of power, stupidity, and perversion. Macabre collective pathologies. Fear. Apathy. Depersonalization. Rhinocerization (in Ionesco's terms). The demon of sadism and stubborn stupidity.

Where are the limits of self-preservation, how much can the human being endure, and to what transformations is he prepared to succumb—willingly or under terror? Fear, exhaustion, disgust— at work, standing in lines, reading the same stupid newspaper all over again, watching the two hours of daily nausea on television. The registration of typewriters with the police, the underequipped and overused clinics, the feeling that you could die at any moment, and that every hour of survival merely retards, prolongs, dismembers this slow dying, day after day, week after week. You would gradually stop seeing your friends because the buses ran very infrequently and were overcrowded, and it had become impossible to get from one end of the city to the other, and because you had nothing—food, drink, or even cigarettes—to offer them when they came to visit. Because you were sick of repeating the same lament for the billionth time, and because you didn't want to face the other's defeat—marked each time by new wrinkles—and recognize it as your own.

And the lie became more insolent by the day. Despair confined by neurosis. Resignation poisoned by cynicism. These were only the most obvious manifestations of a multifaceted social condition whose paradoxically destructive coherence mocked all attempts at logical explanation. A general picture borne out by any random sequence of personal events, the raw materials of biography.

The first half of 1986 involved me in an exhausting struggle with the censors, who had put a halt to the printing of my novel *Plicul negru* (*The Black Envelope*). A fight with a stubborn, demonic adversary who kept inventing fresh and absurd demands. Half a year of daily wrangling over particular pages, sentences, words.

In May, I took part in a colloquium ("The Contemporary Romanian Novel") in the Transylvanian town of Tîrgu-Mureş. My friendly relations with colleagues at the literary journal sponsoring the colloquium persuaded me to accept the invitation. Ever since the explosive Writers' Conference of 1981, the official procedure for all writers' meetings was as follows: suppress all contacts with the public (even the brief press reports about these events had to be cryptic and disinformative), tape-record all comments, frustrate all demands, send all proposals to be "checked" by the security organs whose job it is to update the dossier of each of the participants.

Present at the conference, in addition to the fifteen or twenty writers who had been invited, was a delegation of the Bucharest

Council for Socialist Culture and Education, some local cultural activists and party functionaries, as well as several unknown figures whose appearance and bearing betrayed the Institution to which they belonged. On the conference table, naturally, stood a tape recorder.

I was determined not to speak. And yet, listening to the all-too-clever and sly arguments of a talented colleague about the primacy of the aesthetic as the only legitimate literary criterion, I couldn't restrain myself. I contradicted his statements about the irrelevance of politically tendentious "ballast" and tried to show that, on the contrary, the "aesthetic" retreat from everyday life with its urgent issues explained why contemporary Romanian literature had not yet produced a very large number of major novels. Perhaps because "aesthetics" had not become "East-ethics?"[2]

My use of this pun was, of course, not unconsidered; nor was my concluding reference to Borges and Sábato. I was careful not to make explicit reference to the similarities between Argentina and Romania, which were very much on my mind in those days. I am referring not just to similarities of structure and temperament but also to the chasm between tremendous artistic potential and the most sinister political reality. (While writing *The Black Envelope*, I was engaged in a steady internal dialogue not only with the obscure and strange organization of the blind in Ernesto Sábato's novel *On Heroes and Tombs* but also with the Argentine dictatorship.)

The next day, just before my flight back to Bucharest, an editor of the local literary review warned me in confidence that a State Security officer had visited him and some of his colleagues that morning to ask them for their opinion about my comment at the colloquium and, in general, about my character.

There were four of us on the way to the airport. At the control booth, we had to show our tickets and our papers. A routine check—the three with whom I was traveling were already on their way to the gate—but lo and behold, I was singled out for special

---

[2] The Romanian language allows the punning reference to *est* (east) in the word *estetica*.

treatment. The officer on duty took my papers. "Just checking," he said. My three colleagues turned around and waited in solidarity with me for my case to be resolved. The explanations given us by the soldiers at the gate displayed nothing more than ordinary hostile behavior of men in uniform toward civilians.

"Routine procedure," a friend and connoisseur of this kind of provocation would later explain to me. "Nothing important, really. They just wanted to let you know they've got their eye on you. Which you should have suspected anyway."

Sometime in the next few weeks I applied for a trip to the West as a tourist. I had unofficially heard that I had been awarded a fellowship for the next year at the DAAD Künstlerprogramm in West Berlin. The Romanian postal "service" had (of course) made sure that the official letter of invitation did not reach me—which, paradoxically, turned out to my advantage. Had I received the letter, I would never have been granted permission to be in West Berlin for a year, since these types of permission are given—or rather, as a rule, refused—at the highest level of the country's hierarchy.[3]

There were many people at the local police precinct in charge of foreign travel that day in June. I had time to read the bulletin boards in the waiting room. One displayed the mug shots of delinquents and described the infractions they had perpetrated—three young men who had been accomplices in an incident of assault and theft. The captions under their pictures were virtually identical: so-and-so, born in such and such a place, without occupation, no previous criminal record, has committed, in complicity with so-and-so, assault and theft against such and such a citizen, and has been taken into custody for the purpose of due punishment. This text, full of grammatical errors, was repeated under each of the frowning and head-shaved young faces, with one exception: the last and youngest,

[3] Scientific exchanges and research trips in Romania fell under the auspices of the National Council for Science and Technology, headed by Elena Ceauşescu, President Ceauşescu's wife and number two in command of the country.

aged sixteen, was described not just as "without occupation," but as a "Gypsy without occupation." This in a police district station in the year 1986! Hanging next to numerous posters full of citations from the constitution of the "multilaterally developed" society, which, everyone knew, made ethnic discrimination or incitement to such discrimination a punishable offense.

In the middle of October I found in my mailbox the miraculous notification, stamped as "special" by the Ministry of the Interior— my permission to travel! It was hard to fend off the hysteria that follows in the wake of euphoria, the sensation that you are being shadowed at every step, an uncertainty that makes you a plaything for the sadistic entertainment of the authorities, who are fully capable of annulling the validity of their own permits.

If misfortunes never come alone, happy events sometimes come in bunches also. In the next few days I learned that my book *Pe contur* (*On the Fringes*) had been awarded a prize by the Writers' Union, which had just convened to choose the best books published in 1984.[4] Just a few years earlier, I had been exposed to vicious attacks in retaliation for my public critique of a neofascist editorial that had been published in the goonishly nationalist "cultural" weekly of the Bucharest Communist Party Council. So my pleasure at receiving the prize was tempered by a certain degree of mistrust.

In November, I took the train to my native town of Suceava in the north, to say good-bye to my parents before traveling abroad. Sharing my compartment, opposite my reserved seat, was a passenger in a suit and tie, with no baggage other than an attaché case, very deeply absorbed in reading a newspaper—the "shadow" that had to accompany me to my destination, and perhaps further ("just to let you know they've got their eye on you").

There were giant posters all over the city: DAYS OF CULTURE IN SUCEAVA. First a day of music, then a day of sculpture, then of

---

[4] Awarding prizes in 1986 for books published in 1984 was one of the less bizarre aspects of the activities of the Romanian Writers' Union, which was strangled by the fact that even the most ordinary actions had to first be approved by "higher organs."

literature, film, theater, etc. The names of those who were to engage in dialogue with the stars from Bucharest had been chosen according to the recently established sandwich system: for the sake of calculated confusion, pair a genuine writer with a talentless blowhard, an opportunistic scoundrel with an honorable artist—and you have a legitimate combination, fully approved.

On that cold and dreary autumn day, as I headed for the grocery store to see which food line I might join, I couldn't have cared less for this "cultural" event. This was the city of my childhood and my youth, and my only purpose in being here was to savor it as much as I could before departing.

But I was stopped by a neighbor, a local journalist. He was going to the literary event and insisted that I go with him. I was embarrassed. There was a humbly reproachful hint that I was keeping myself aloof, not just from the literary and political scene but also from my former associates and colleagues, evidently because I considered them provincial. He seemed positively hurt, and I unfortunately gave in.

When I found myself in the office of the director of the local House of Culture, where the Party activists and local journalists were already assembled, I felt even more awkward and strange. Unshaven, tired, preoccupied, wearing a crumpled sweater, I stood as a real intruder among men and women who had dressed for the festive occasion. But the director seemed delighted that my unexpected presence would add a "well-known novelist" to the panel discussion ("Tradition and Innovation in Contemporary Romanian Literature"). I objected that my name had not been announced on the posters, that I had nothing to say on this topic, that I wasn't even dressed for the occasion. He would not accept a refusal. It was too late.

Soon the "Bucharest writers" made their appearance. Instead of the seven who had been announced, there were three. Actually only two, as one was introduced as a journalist of the Communist Youth newspaper *Scînteia Tineretului.*

A poet, a critic, a novelist—an ideal trio for the panel. We went up on the stage and sat down. The audience consisted of fifty people, most of them children between ten and fifteen, and about ten teachers from the local schools. It was agreed that we would take questions from the audience to simplify the discussion. Many minutes passed before anyone plucked up the courage to break the silence. This gave me time to observe the children squirming in their seats, wearing winter coats and fur hats, and their teachers, also in coats and hats; for the auditorium was, needless to say, unheated—a fact that would have been a far more appropriate subject of discussion than the state of contemporary Romanian literature.

An elderly lady, looking like an Austrian housemaid, in a thick gray overcoat cut in military style and hunting cap tilted at a coquettish angle, launched the first question: "What's going on with the Nobel Prize? Why haven't we got a Nobel Prize? Why has no Romanian writer ever received the Nobel Prize?"

The brilliant poet, aroused by the childishness of the question, displayed his ironic verve but then passed the essentially unanswered question to his friend. Without excess of modesty, the professor confessed that he had been for many years Romania's consultant to the Nobel Foundation (a fact he had never divulged in public before), went on to mention his frequent trips to the West and his friendly relations with various literary figures of world stature, and decried the commercialization of culture in the West and the unfair way in which the world treated non-Western and particularly Romanian culture. And then came the surprise ending that was the goal of all his meandering: "A few years ago, Saul Bellow visited us here. When I met him I asked him: 'Tell me, sir, who is behind you? Who is backing you? Who actually gave you your Nobel Prize?' " The pubescent audience and the apathetic educators suddenly showed visible signs of life inside their heavy coats and beneath the fur hats they had pulled tightly over their ears.

The speaker prolonged the strategic pause a bit, then resumed his aria: "These are the facts. Someone is pulling strings, let's face it. Why not place a finger on the open wound? Nelly Sachs is an absolutely mediocre poet. And these Jews . . . all these Jews write in old languages that no one understands." He turned to the poet, asking him for help: "What's his name, the one who got the Nobel Prize a few years ago?"

The poet leapt to his assistance: "Bashevis Singer."

Enlightened, the professor found his stride again. "Exactly, Singer, that's the one. I found a few books by this Singer in translation. I read them very closely, and I can assure you: absolutely worthless. He's certainly not a writer."

I was not, under the circumstances, in the mood to defend the merits of such an eloquent witness as Nelly Sachs or a writer as interesting as Isaac Bashevis Singer. Nevertheless, I felt obliged to qualify the professor's all-too-categorical statements. I pointed out the difference between athletic achievements, which are established by the precise measurement of inches and seconds, and works of art, which are difficult to evaluate with perfect objectivity. Literary awards, I said, are rarely perfect calls, and this holds as true for the Romanian Writers' Union as it does for the Nobel Foundation. The judgment need only be plausible—that is, it must fall within a certain zone of artistic merit. Hankering for prizes, in any case, is a sign of frustration, and frustration in no way stimulates artistic creativity, which requires solitude and originality, not honors and publicity.

I reminded the professor of our having met, several years before, at a literary conference in Belgrade where our hosts overwhelmed us not only with volumes by Yugoslav writers that had been translated abroad but also with lengthy biobibliographical tomes, in major languages of international communication, about Yugoslav literature. This, I said, Romania was still unable to offer. The professor nodded in agreement, but I was not at all sure he remembered those days in Belgrade, for I had often seen him dead drunk, bereft of the good-natured mask he assumed for his hypocritical speeches about freedom of speech and the end of censorship in Romania.[5]

---

[5] In the late 1970s the Romanian censorship organ, Direcţia Presei, was dissolved. Censorship, however, did not end but was diffused, passing into the hands of individual editors,

After a few more questions and answers, the professor informed the audience about the projects of the publishing house he directed. He complained at some length of the problems confronting a Romanian editor, but stressed the paternal care and support for culture shown by the country's president, the secretary general of the Party, whom he had had the honor of meeting on several occasions, and of whose generous and farsighted views on culture and art he had personally apprised himself. And then, once again, an astonishing finale.

"Nevertheless," he said, "new obstacles keep arising. Let's face the truth squarely. Why pretend? A few years ago I was visited by two professors from Israel. I knew them. They were formerly from Romania. They asked me: 'What are you doing with the Eminescu[6] edition? Is it out yet?' 'Well, no,' I replied, 'and it's your fault. Your chief rabbi's behind the delay, if you really want to know.' And that is the truth. Let's not mince words!"

Leaving the auditorium after the debate, I expressed to the poet my indignation at the cynical behavior of the professor. To speak that way in front of a roomful of children, in secret agreement with the local cultural officials, and spread such shameless lies! Anti-Western and anti-Semitic Party propaganda! When he knows perfectly well that cultural institutions in the West aren't all dominated by political interests, that all Western culture isn't perverted and commercial, and that the complete edition of Eminescu is not being delayed just because of his anti-Semitic texts but also because of his anti-Russian texts and other, more complex reasons. How vile! To exploit the trust of children like that! Instead of explaining to them

---

periodicals, etc. In the mid-1980s a central censorship organ was reinstituted, a *lectorat* within the Council for Socialist Culture and Education, i.e., a group to oversee and advise the individual editors. This amounted to a stricter form of control than before. Now there was double censorship—self-censorship by the writers, who could expect to be held accountable for their decisions, and censorship by the control forum appointed to check up on them.

[6] Mihai Eminescu, the Romanian national poet, a great artist with a conservative, at times nationalistic political vision.

why it is they don't have enough to eat and why it's so cold in their homes and in that auditorium!

The young poet, already not so young, did not allow himself to be contaminated by my naive indignation. He made a calm-down gesture with his hand and reminded me that the professor had earned his stripes in the service of a certain higher cause. I knew the "institution" he was referring to, but still I did not understand why what had just happened was therefore negligible.

"It's silliness, small potatoes," he said. "It's not worth talking about, it's really not worth talking about."

When I told my friends in Bucharest about my experience, they were no less outraged than I was. But at the Council for Socialist Culture and Education, the Suceava incident was being considered from a very different point of view: an investigatory commission was set up to determine who had given me the illegitimate authority to present my views at the conference, in defiance of the council's exclusive jurisdiction in such matters.

I had known for many years the idiotic fear and hypocritical sadism of Party functionaries appointed to "cultural" work. I had felt it more than once, like so many others. Nevertheless, I was shocked to learn, two months after that literary colloquium in Suceava when I was already abroad, that "for ideological reasons" the Council for Socialist Culture and Education had revoked the prize recently awarded by the Writers' Union to my *Pe contur.* Then it all came back to me: the debilitating war with the censors, the vicious press campaign against me, the incident at the airport in Tîrgu-Mureş, the House of Culture in Suceava, and along with these personal memories, Eugène Ionesco's small text: "In Legionnaire, bourgeois, nationalist Romania I saw the demon of sadism and stubborn stupidity incarnate before me."

It was still as true as ever. Only the first two terms would have to be changed. It was no longer Legionnaire but socialist Romania. And the demon was no longer incarnate in the bourgeoisie but in the State Security apparatus.

I I

For some time there has been much talk about Central Europe. To the extent that the discussion of this still vaguely defined notion is not dominated by an exclusive club mentality but rather by a search for an inclusive, cooperative solution, the long-term prospects for this part of Europe could be truly spectacular. But even in the absence of a clear definition of its key term, the debate is of burning interest.

In his excellent article "Does Central Europe Exist?" (*New York Review of Books,* October 9, 1986), Timothy Garton Ash analyzes the opinions of Havel, Michnik, and Konrad on the subject, showing their defining criteria to be based on cultural tradition and stages of development instead of geography. (Tomáš Masaryk, for instance, included in his definition the Scandinavians and Baltic peoples, along with Poles, Czechs, Slovaks, Magyars, Serbo-Croatians, Romanians, Bulgarians, Albanians, Greeks, and Turks, but excluded Germans and Austrians since they chose to place Europe's center in Berlin and Vienna respectively.)

If "membership" in Central Europe is essentially a spiritual matter, then our point of departure should be the "distinctive skepticism"—"a bit mysterious, a bit nostalgic, often tragic, and even at times heroic"—that Havel refers to in "The Anatomy of Reticence," but also the *"kulturpolitische Antihypothese"* proposed by Konrad, for whom the Central European spirit belongs to the "rational, humanist, democratic, skeptical, and tolerant" West. And in the analysis, both Havel's and Konrad's views converge in that "civil society" for which Michnik pleads.

Given these premises, Romania could present convincing arguments for belonging to Central Europe. Unfortunately, "real socialism" in Romania abused the European norm in important ways. Especially during the 1970s and 1980s, this country reminded one not only of China's and North Korea's "proletarian dictatorships," or of Latin America's right-wing dictatorships, but also of long-ago periods of despotic barbarism that bequeathed to our times what we typically think of as Balkan "underdevelopment." Painfully I recall the words of the musician Georges Enesco: "If only our administration and politics were on the same level as the arts, we would be one of the happiest countries on earth."

Skepticism has always been a Romanian trait, especially in people's attitudes toward politics and politicians, and usually toward the very idea of political engagement.

The mediocrity of so many contemporary political leaders in both large and small countries, the moral duplicity that reveals itself in their rhetoric, can only reinforce that skepticism. Eventually it degenerates into indifference and contempt.

A national history consisting of a series of catastrophes, a geographic position at the crossroads of East and West, directly in the path—and at the mercy—of interests more powerful than one's own: all this probably teaches caution. What can you do? You have to survive. Do you become a fatalist? Do you develop an acutely suspicious ear? Do you gamble and play? Your volatile temper is spiced by humor and muted by that quality of *bun simț*,[7] for which you are famous, which owes much more to an archaic, pagan, instinctual wisdom than it does to the constructs of ideology, be it religious or atheistic. Romanians like to repeat, often with an undertone of regret and even of guilt, "We haven't produced any saints"—or, in ironic self-exculpation, "The Romanian is born a poet."

Caution toward ideologies and suspicion toward politics do not, however, necessarily lead to moral stability. The noncommittal stance doesn't only have positive effects. Among its frequent consequences are, unfortunately, compromise and complicity. The defor-

---

[7] Literally, "good sense." The phrase connotes a kind of instinctual delicacy in human relations, an unaffected, spontaneous sense of tact and decency. The German word *Menschlichkeit* is perhaps close in meaning.

mation of high principle to the point of caricature can discredit faith in principles as such. The social mechanism imperceptibly begins to function in the good old "natural" ways, by mutual favors and force of circumstance, proliferating corruption, Byzantinism, demagogy, abuse of power, and nepotism on a truly fantastic scale. Under these conditions, what is normally called life is pushed into the background and locked in a system of ciphers and codes.

There were press reports in 1986 that in a park in Zagreb, Yugoslavia, a young intellectual made a mimed protest speech before a crowd that had gathered spontaneously, a speech without words (to avoid being accused of breaking the law). It seems, however, that the audience understood his message perfectly. In Romania, this coded type of communication—in response to the brutal machinery of repression—permeated the whole of society, not just private relationships. Precise knowledge of a system of signs—perceptible only to initiates, and often implied rather than expressed—was indispensable in any exchange between individuals and groups. A whole society, under surveillance around the clock, split between feigned submission and masked refusal.

While working on my novel *The Black Envelope,* especially in the description of the association of deaf-mutes, which I had conceived as a pseudosocialist equivalent of the evil organization of the blind in Ernesto Sábato's *On Heroes and Tombs,* I was forced to meditate at length on this theme of coded communication.

The censorship's brutal and repeated intervention reduced my book to a system of coded innuendos inaccessible to all but the most sophisticated readers, except for the details that refer obviously (though still in code) to the banalities of daily life. The mysterious mark that begins to appear on the faces of one's fellow citizens, a scar right next to the eyebrow, refers to a certain overused wink that at all levels of the hierarchy serves as a signal of mutual accord; and, of course, in the book it serves as a reference to every sort of hidden and compulsive signal—a sort of nation-wide tic.

I visited the Bucharest association of deaf-mutes. I was shocked by the miserable condition of the handicapped in a handicapped country: here was the extreme limit of the social and moral crisis in which the whole population had been plunged. I was also horrified by the cynicism of the authorities, who saw fit to oppress even this suffering minority to the point of complete mental and moral degradation. The deaf-mutes' newspaper in Bucharest was in no way different in language and layout from *Scînteia*[8] or from any provincial Party publication. Perhaps it was no accident that it was called *Our Life.*

The traditional mistrust in those who govern, the gulf between leaders and led, had grown to grotesque proportions in the last decade. Politics and politicians were seen as embodiments of stupidity or baseness (usually in combination), always surrounded by the aura of the ridiculous.

Everything political seemed tainted—not only those in authority, but sometimes even their opposition. Those who committed themselves politically on one side or the other were automatically suspected of some petty personal motive masquerading as high principle. It is no wonder that under such conditions sensible people stayed away from politics and even from the serious discussion of politics. The nonpolitical stance thus became a refuge, a safe retreat, since one's abstention was not declared openly, and one became active only in exceptional instances.

The reproach of passivity frequently leveled at Romania was, however, only partially justified. Of course one cannot speak of a revolutionary tradition in Romania, but one shouldn't forget that in no other European socialist country has surveillance been as total and repression as severe.

The lack of revolutionary tradition is evident even in the scarcity of noteworthy uprisings and rebellions in recent Romanian history. The peasant revolt of 1907 and some of the workers' strikes in the

---

[8] *Scînteia* was the Communist party daily and the largest newspaper in Romania.

twenties and thirties were simple explosions resulting from intolerable conditions. Nevertheless, there were revolts. The miners' strike in 1977 and the protest demonstration in Braşov in 1987—an officially organized election-day march that shifted abruptly into unrestrained popular fury against the officials—were not the only events of this kind. Smaller eruptions evaporated in the absence of any support or response from abroad. They had little chance of success in any case.

The spontaneous character of collective revolts was replicated in the outbursts of individuals as well. Yet it is worth noting that, among the relatively few Romanian dissidents, many were Party members—which means that at least part of the time, and with reservations, they were willing to come to terms with the system.

More often than not, the decision to break with the system took place in a fit of rage. A dissenter was immediately confronted with the fact that he stood alone and could not count on support from anyone. Recovery of one's courage and dignity often set in when one's despair, unhappiness, and indignation at the general misery could no longer be endured. But the expression of social outrage usually remained limited to private explosions. For years there was a lack of any public discussion, for years the whole nation was exposed to the repressive monotony of primitive, demagogic, cynical Party jargon and to quick repression by the Securitate. Could that be why even the most virulent protests had an improvisatory, rhetorical character?

Caragiale, the great Romanian playwright, wrote about this flaw: "We are all irritable, but only a few of us are expressive." The comment is witty but it does not explain much. The real reason why most attempts at opposing the Romanian regime were dissipated in improvised, transient, isolated explosions was the virtual impossibility of establishing the very foundations of genuine social dialogue. Even with the recovery of a more democratic way of life, Romania will probably suffer profoundly in the future from this dark and long period of terror.

Of all the countries that might claim membership in Central

Europe, Romania is probably the least talented for communism. Paradoxical as it may seem, it is precisely the absence of a revolutionary tradition that explains the catastrophic, "un-European" situation in the Romania of the last two decades.

In 1945 the Romanian Communist party had no more than a thousand members.[9] It is easy to see why now, in the 1980s, at the last stage of the masquerade, that is, after four decades of Communist politics and administration, it would be hard to find a thousand authentic Communists in Romania. Unfortunately, it has also become relatively easy to see why, under these conditions, Romania under Ceauşescu had almost four million Communist party members.[10] Per capita it may have had the largest Communist party in the world!

The Party card represented nothing more than a certificate of adaptation, a proof of one's social normalcy that was added to all the other documents in one's personal record. To inflate a party to such proportions is tantamount to annulling it. This might have been interpreted as the outcome of a sane and intelligent strategy if the power once held by the Party had not long since passed into the hands of State Security. The advantages of Party membership were of a purely potential kind; they depended on the individual's opportunistic energy and on the cynicism that comes to the aid of the instinct for self-preservation.

The situation could take on grotesque, tragicomic forms. It would be hard, for example, to forget the commotion surrounding the Romanian publication of Mircea Eliade's *History of Religious Beliefs and Ideas* in 1981. The oddness of this event was exacerbated by the book's title in an officially atheistic country at a time when the censors were frenzied by strict orders with regard to anything resembling religion. What gave the contradiction a near-scandalous aura was the well-known fact that Eliade had belonged to the

---

[9] Michael Shafir, *Romania* (Boulder: Lynne Rienner Publications, 1985), p. 27.

[10] Over 3.5 million was the official figure quoted often in the Romanian press in recent years.

extreme right before the war, and that after the war he had deserted to "American imperialism."

The book's relatively small edition added to the general excitement: interested readers had to hustle for a "connection" in a bookstore, and naturally many were unable to secure a copy of the book. Actually the edition wasn't all that small—there was even a second printing—but most copies were sold through the hierarchy's "special channels." Obtaining *The History of Religious Beliefs and Ideas* was the privilege of those who called themselves atheists and revolutionaries, sworn enemies of all renegades and imperialists, etc., etc.

"If only our administration and politics were on the same level as the arts," there would presumably have been far fewer Party members per capita in Romania. Even in recent years, when applying for membership in the Party had become a routine gesture—or perhaps especially then—the percentage of Party members among writers fell far below the national average, even though the Party never tired of asserting and proving its leading role in the Writers' Union, as in all other institutions. And the proportion was even lower among writers of real value—by which I mean those who were faithful to their vocation, who preserved their identity, and whose works, though written in a coded language, were unequivocally opposed to Romania's administration and policies under Ceauşescu. Therefore the population looked to the honest and gifted writers and artists with high esteem and trust even when they were silenced.

The last Writers' Union conference, which took place in 1981,[11] was a genuine form of revolt. Had the speeches made then become known to the public, people would have been surprised, to say the least, at the vigor and frankness with which writers spoke out about Romania's crippled cultural life.

---

[11] Although the Romanian Writers' Union was supposed to meet in conference every four years (according to the statutes approved by the Party itself), no such meeting of writers has been allowed since 1981.

"Misplaced Europeans" is how one contemporary Romanian novelist defines his compatriots (reminiscent of Borges's "The Argentinean is an exiled European"). But Romanians have always had an astounding capacity for regeneration, for finding the strength to recuperate rapidly in the uncertain intervals between disasters. And forms of life, of creation, of resistance in Romania often sustained themselves—as far as was possible under this cruel, savage dictatorship—through culture.

I I I

On receiving the literary prize of the city of Bremen, Paul Celan emphasized that he came from a little-known landscape, "a country inhabited by people and books." Celan was referring to the Bukovina of his adolescence, but these words could apply to Romania as a whole.

Paul Celan came from cosmopolitan Bukovina, where Romanians, Jews, Germans, Poles, and Ukrainians lived together in an area that vibrated with a special spiritual atmosphere. Constantin Brâncuşi comes from poor Oltenia, the "land of quick thoughts and words," Georges Enesco from that lyrical and charming part of Moldavia that is considered "the placenta of Romanian culture." The iconoclast philosopher Emil Cioran was born in Răşinari, a typical Romanian village in southern Transylvania, not far from the German-founded *burg* of Sibiu, a city with a distinctly Central European air, and Eugène Ionesco is a child of Bucharest, that metropolis glittering with irony and elegance, where misery is disguised as paradox and sarcasm as bantering cordiality. Panait Istrati is the child of a port on the Danube over which float the shining mirages of freedom and infinite space. Romania—a disconcerting mixture of contrasts: the Turk and the Tartar from the moonscape of torrid Dobruja, the competent yeoman from Banat, where so many Swabians found themselves a new fatherland, or the Saxons of Transylvania in their centuries-old dialogue with Hungarians and Romanians.

But the nostalgia that writes these lines remembers not only the fishing village[12] where summer vacations among friends and the closeness of the sea seemed almost to cancel the sadness of the whole year, or the Carpathian forests that awakened such grandiose reveries in me when I was an adolescent; it runs back also to the young peasant woman who braved both war and the freezing wind of the Ukrainian steppes to save us, and to friends to whom literature has remained the Archimedean point and the North Star; to the vanished years when first love and the city library were my best schools; to my mother's fresh grave. This longing is for every-thing—people and books, suffering, hope, rebellion—that animates that irreplaceable realm we call a human life.

Anyone visiting Romania in the last decade could hardly imagine the hospitable beauty of the country and the vital, spirited charm its everyday life once possessed; and I don't mean only the brief, relatively peaceful period between the two wars, when Romania was striving for democracy, or only the few, all too transient thaws of the postwar period.

During the relatively "liberal" decade of 1965–75, Romania was by no means prosperous, nor can one say that people's everyday lives were permitted to unfold spontaneously and naturally. Yet the memory of that time has a tonic vibrancy: that allegro humming of sprightly Latinity, of wit and melodious decorum; you could move more freely, speak more freely about people and books. It was as if, overnight, people and books had risen from the dead—congenial talk, glittering parties, melancholy strolls, the excitement of ventur-ing on some project, all this had come back to life. The new climate was not, as in other socialist countries, a reactivation of political involvement in response to a policy shift on the part of the leader-

---

[12] I am referring to 2 Mai, a fishing village on the Bulgarian border that became a chic but unpretentious resort for the Bucharest intelligentsia. People either camped in tents by the sea or boarded with the families of local fishermen. Since 1982, the construction of a military port nearby, restrictions on camping, and the arrest and unexplained death of one of the 2 Mai regulars (whose personal journal was used against him) have made this a much less inviting spot for many.

ship; it was a brief opportunity to set aside the government's political agenda and return to the simple enjoyment of life, in a country where people have always preferred songs to prayers and solemn oaths. That period stimulated economic initiative only to a negligible degree, but its benefit to art and literature extended into the next decade. We took advantage of any small chance to be in touch with the arts and the movements of thought in the West, and it was possible to take a somewhat independent position on social and political issues, and to express it in one's own personal style.

Glasnost was, in Romania, the implicit program of art and literature, before the terror of a frightened, hysterical censorship stifled it in recent years. The cultural landscape remained fragmented and discordant. Many Romanian books exhibited real expressive power and critical consciousness. Of course, as in every totalitarian state, you could also find many demonstrations of the most abject cynicism and opportunism, especially among the "official" (established) writers and those still striving for the laurels of state approval. But for a convincing and reliable diagnosis of the country's spiritual condition, one needed only compare the official writers' demagogic declarations of fealty to their rulers with the disgust that is expressed between the lines in their books.

The Janus-head mentality creates some bizarre situations. For many years one could watch, in the press and on television, the spectacular performances of a cynical and well-paid poet, a sort of state-sponsored disc jockey who liked to serve up all the favorite tunes of power—the folk song, the patriotic march, the ode to the Führer—until one day he fell into disgrace and vanished. Harder to understand, especially in times of misery and despair, was the series performed for the system by an old and celebrated philosopher who, after years of monastic seclusion, allowed his own extremely right-wing ideas, for which he had been imprisoned for years, to receive official sanction because they offered the leaders a new legitimacy.

For some writers, fashioning slogans and inane propagandistic metaphors was "merely" a routine; in other cases, this practice entailed a much more serious form of degradation.

Well-known writers even agreed to lend their pens or the journals they edited to the service of the State Security. They poisoned
the cultural atmosphere and persecuted their blacklisted colleagues
with tireless, diabolical energy. The future chronicles of our present
history will list the names of a number of "Romanian artists" and
"Romanian writers" among those who left an indelible stain on the
country.

And what about the others? The ones who maintained a proud
silence or exploded with suicidal rage? The many honest and talented artists, writers, and intellectuals who resisted? And what
about those who showed their contempt for politics, their aloofness
from power, their improvised elitist self-isolation, their disdainful
withdrawal from the struggles of the *vulgus*?

The fundamental condition of those who were honest, those who
resisted, was a protracted state of latent explosion. In a culture
obsessed with aesthetics and favoring an ironic aloofness from
ethical imperatives, in a Romania devastated by compromise and
complicity, where neither books nor people had a voice, a genuine
writer could not in the long run endure the aggression that philistin-
ism and cowardice fostered all around him. What sort of commitment could one ask of him? An unwavering faith in the primacy of
the aesthetic as the prerequisite for ethical engagement? Aesthetics
as East-ethics, then? The pun found more than one echo. A recent
novel by an author of the younger generation ends with the exclamation: "I need this East-ethics!" The unhappiness, the frustration,
and the humiliation became more and more explosive, not just for
the intellectuals but for the entire country.

Adaptability, skeptical pragmatism, and jovial resignation dominated Romanian reality for a very long time, to the detriment of
political engagement, coherent resistance, and constructive energy.
Romanian—and naturally not just Romanian—beauty is more
easily found in the individual than in the collective, behind the
scenes rather than on center stage, in the dubious and roundabout
solution (often preservative of some amply human resource) than

in the firmness and clarity of a fixed position. After all, goodness is quiet and modest, it has trouble shielding itself against the noise and aggression of evil; truth, too, survives in fractured, equivocal forms, and finds refuge in obscurity and ingenious codes.

People and books . . . It seemed that an indestructible hedonism had always animated the people and the books of the Romanian landscape. A paradoxical priority was given to the immediacy of human relations, and also to relationships with landscapes and all the other existential pleasures that are the gift of a friendly climate. Paradoxical not because of the ineluctable contradictions of human interaction, but because of an occasional suspension of essential moral criteria.

Recently I talked to an American intellectual who knows Romania well. I asked him what he found most surprising about the country. "Human relationships," he said. "The relationship between the 'good' and the 'bad,' if I may use these conventional terms. The abyss between good and evil people—or, more precisely, between those who feel drawn to human principles and those in the voluntary service of evil—seems nowhere to be greater. And yet they cooperate. I can't imagine a stranger, more puzzling collaboration."

Many Romanians considered this paradox—perhaps quite rightly—the result of a humanizing process rooted in that famous *bun simț* that is often cited as the foremost feature of the national character, a mode of communication that limits itself to the domestic and earthy zone of daily existence. But the authorities banked on this self-limitation; they manipulated it. In a society that permitted differences of opinion only in the private sphere, all the impulses that elsewhere would lead to frank argument or expression of tolerance instead generated discord, dishonesty, indifference, and an apathy that irritated the rulers whenever one of the so-called grandiose projects miscarried, but that suited them very nicely when it got in the way of a united and collective movement of revolt.

It is true that, even during the hardest times, Romanians have known how to build enclaves in which reason and normalcy could be preserved. Culture was perhaps the most important of these enclaves. Unfortunately, after the war the gulf widened between word and deed, between professed and genuine conviction, between political theater and social reality.

During the last decade, this "sad country blessed with humor," as one of her great poets called her, was presenting herself, as so often in times of crisis and collapse, with a host of oppressive questions.

The disaster was absolute: the evil had to all appearances silenced the good. A whole nation subjugated, hungry, humiliated, and forced to celebrate the crime ceaselessly. People and books alike thrown into the abyss. A country that destroyed its own monuments, its own memories; that was undergoing its own "racial purification" with the emigration of its last Jews, the massive departure of its German population, and the escalating conflict with the Magyar minority; a country that was making the megalomaniacal claim—like some other great nations with a rich cultural heritage at similar junctures of imminent collapse—of a glorious lineage reaching back some two thousand years; a country whose plans for more "multilateral development" extended into the next millennium, in blind disregard of our unstable nuclear era; a country that was governed by the dictator and his police like a penal colony, and that promised to gradually transform all its citizens into hardworking, infantile, submissive wage slaves for the sake of future penal colonies, two thousand more years of stumbling through the dark, of multilateral degeneration.

At the end of an age that brought so many peoples the end of colonialism—and with it their entry into their own history—Romania seemed about to depart from history altogether.

Washington, D.C.
October 1988
Translated by Irina Livezeanu and Joel Agee

POSTSCRIPTUM

In December 1989, the darkest dictatorship was at last overturned, but the speed and difficulties surrounding the changes in Eastern Europe have taught us to be careful with our prophesy. A new beginning can only be made if the healing of wounds does not ignore the country's history of moral ambiguity, in a half-century suffocated by dictatorships of both Left and Right.

A decade ago, one of the leaders of Solidarity, Leszeka Moczulski, gave a severe definition of dissidence, arguing: "We are not dissidents. That term insults the opposition in Poland. Dissidents are those who broke with the Communist party because they were disillusioned." However, we can suggest a looser understanding of the term when applied to Romania, because in the harsher totalitarian climate of that country, any sign of *life* whatsoever was tantamount to a sign of resistance, of opposition, and thus, by implication, of dissidence.

A movement like Solidarity would have been unthinkable in Romania, where there was no Catholic church, no revolutionary tradition, and a dictatorship oppressive in the extreme. There were, of course, many Communists who became disillusioned with the Party, some even becoming dissidents, but the large majority—particularly those (too many) who had joined the Party in the seventies and eighties—were neither dissidents nor believers. They were the sort of opportunists that characterized the "real socialism" of the last decades.

The ever increasing terror, misery, and frustration of the last years did, however, lead to a significant rise in the number of the regime's opponents. It was not a complete surprise when, in the miraculous convergence of events that culminated in the December revolt, these people—the students especially—displayed a courage clearly long pent up.

*   *   *

But before that December, in the absence of the kind of direct
political resistance witnessed in other Eastern bloc countries, it was
primarily only the artist who was left to challenge the Romanian
regime—doing so indirectly through culture. A significant number
of Romanian writers never wanted and never accepted membership
in the Party's canon. They understood that their role as artists
demanded that they maintain a critical distance from the system.
When asked if he would become a Party member, a leading
Romanian writer of the older generation answered: "I can't. I am
already a Party of one. I am a writer."

In no other European socialist country (except perhaps Albania)
was surveillance as total and repression as prompt as in Romania.
Samizdat was not possible in a country where even the use of
typewriters was controlled. But the ambiguous and sly nature of the
Party meant that it often colluded in allowing relative freedom of
literary expression as long as tacitly agreed rules were observed.

"Censorship is the mother of metaphor," wrote Borges, and
truth in Romanian literature was forced to find refuge in obscurity
and ingenious codes, surviving in often equivocal and obscure
forms. The reader expected from literature what he could not find
in newspapers, history books, or sociology. The reader read in
between the lines, and the writer accepted this distortion as the
inevitable price to pay for solidarity with his audience. The process
involved inordinate amounts of energy, inner exile, and sometimes
more. But at least culture allowed for a kind of underground life,
restoring some trust and creativity in thought, beauty, and ideas, a
kind of spiritual dialogue at a time when the ubiquity of the secret
police made real dialogue impossible.

If politics is about power, and art about freedom, then art in a
totalitarian state comes to stand not only as a challenge—as it does
for every authority—it comes to stand for nothing less than the

enemy. To remain honest, to maintain moral and artistic integrity under these circumstances, was something that demanded heroism. And there *were* extreme situations when writers rose above terror, broke with opportunistic local habit, set aside their innate mistrust of rhetoric, and declared a clear opposition against tyranny.

Questions about our past—about the lies, the resistance, the complicity, and about artistic and moral ideals, about honesty and compromise—will remain with us even with the recovery of a more democratic way of life.

We can only wonder what will remain of all the literature that was written in the postwar period in Eastern Europe and if this literature will find the strength for a new beginning in an atmosphere of nonconstraint. We can wonder whether Western consumer society will not soon transform Eastern Europe into part of the global kitsch.

Will television—the daily trivializer—overwhelm cultural life, and will the culture of money be even harder to overcome than the culture of lies? Will J.R. and Sue Ellen replace the pictures of the Romanian dictator on the walls of the country's farmhouses?

"The specific experience I am talking about has given me one great certainty," declared Václav Havel to the U.S. Congress when discussing the changes in his own country. "It is that consciousness precedes being, and not the other way around, as Marxists claim." It is not a conclusion I would agree with: the history of both socialist and capitalist societies shows that the relationship between consciousness and being is far more complicated, and that correspondingly, our conclusion must also be.

Socialism destroyed itself because of its supression of liberty and because of its economic failure. The Marxist prophets were wrong in their prediction that capitalism would be supplanted by socialism-communism; yet in losing the enemy, capitalist society may have to take a more critical approach toward itself, questioning its own successes and failures. In this respect, Havel's words ring true:

"The salvation of this human world lies nowhere else than in the human heart, in the human power to reflect, in human meekness, and in human responsibility."

Bard College
May 1990

ON CLOWNS:
THE DICTATOR
AND THE ARTIST

Notes to a Text by Fellini

The year 1989 did not mark only the bicentennial of the French Revolution, but also the centennials of two figures who—each in his own way—knew how to exploit the hunger of the masses and their vulnerability and gullibility.

"He was a tramp in the big city, using a park bench for a bed. He wore a weathered black derby and a frock coat askew on his shoulders—both tragicomic attempts at respectability. He drifted along the sidewalks, without family. He had no friends. Acquaintances saw him go into strange fits and thought him a clown. But he became a charismatic clown—the center of a show that he perfected and in which he functioned not just as leading man but as writer, director, producer, and set designer. When his little black mustache had become emblematic, when he had grown into the idol of millions, a great Hollywood star called him 'the greatest actor of us all.' His name was Adolf Hitler, born just over a hundred years ago, on April 20, 1889" (Frederic Morton, "Chaplin, Hitler: Outsiders as Actors," *New York Times,* April 24, 1989).

The Hollywood star who was so fascinated by Hitler's histrionic

33

gifts was, of course, Charlie Chaplin, likewise born a hundred years ago, a hundred hours before Hitler. He too was a marginal figure, one of society's outcasts: his father was an alcoholic, his mother was shunted from one charity hospital to another, and the son slept in campgrounds and railroad stations. He was incapable of forming friendships, had difficulties communicating, but would prove to have an irresistible effect on the masses.

Chaplin plays the part of the Dictator in the movie of that name, with its famous scene in which the hero, in a frenzy of triumph, juggles a balloon that represents the globe. The actor emphasizes the grotesque elements in the tyrant's infantile schizophrenia. In its empathy with madness, his acting becomes ambiguously complicitous. The character, initially conceived in a naive, artistic fashion, flips over into a convulsive grimace of demonic ugliness. "Hitler may have been history's most murderous genius, yet his formula shared elements with Chaplin's. Both men tapped the need of the outsider to be let in" (Frederic Morton).

"Do you still collect humorous clippings from the contemporary press similar to those you published in *Auguste the Fool's Apprenticeship Years*?" a writer asked me in an interview that scandalized the official press for months on end: I had said that "the artist cannot dignify officialdom by opposing it in a solemn fashion, because that would mean taking it too seriously and inadvertently reinforcing its authority, thus acknowledging that authority. He pushes the ridiculous to grotesque proportions, but artistically he creates . . . a surfeit of meanings. . . . In today's rushed, confusing society in which everything mixes and is mixed up and destroyed, the ridiculous does run the risk of 'swallowing up' art too. But the artist, even if he has been relegated to the position of a buffoon, tries to assume—even at the price of an apparent, momentary abnegation of the self—an ambiguous stance, to place himself on a shaky seesaw, to transform the loss into a later gain." For me, the artist was an Auguste the Fool; mine was a deep solidarity rather than a superficial empathy with his game and with his destiny.

Where went the proud, romantic image of art with a capital *A*? The artist's situation in the world is that of "Auguste the Fool," *"der arme August,"* as Hans Hartung's father nicknamed his son, clearly intuiting the inner nature of the artist that neither the painter's work nor later life ever overtly disclosed. Aging Thomas Mann, the epitome of a rigorous, serious, and ethical author, saw artists as "eccentric spirits of the ridiculous," "brilliant monks of the absurd," "suspect," and "acrobatic": For him the artist was "neither female nor male, hence not human"; he called him "a grave angel of foolhardiness . . . under the roof of the tent, high above the crowd," performing an aerial balancing act in the great circus of the world.

In the world circus the poet looks like a Knight of the Sad Countenance, an Auguste the Fool ill-equipped for everyday life in which his fellow men offer and receive—according to their efforts, opportunities, and wiles—their share of edible reality. He is a bizarre bungler who dreams of other rules, other evaluations and rewards, and looks for solitary compensations for the role he has been saddled with whether he likes it or not.

Nevertheless, he often demonstrates a deep and hence surprising knowledge of his fellow citizens, with whom he seems to communicate only superficially, and from whom he takes and to whom he returns a kind of magic that is as calculated as it is spontaneous; there are sequences the citizens can recognize even when they appear mysterious and, on the surface, difficult—not always understood, even by himself. His weakness suddenly may be seen as an unconventional and devious strength, his solitude as a deeper kind of solidarity; his imagination becomes a shortcut to reality. One might say that his face is reflected in all the images of the circus that surrounds him, and the mirror turns fast, faster. It is a gift of a moment, a brief shock—a moment of amazement that stuns the entire audience for a fraction of a second.

But what do we see here—the tyrant, part of the troupe of buffoons? Can the frail vagabond (and cultivated man of letters) recognize himself even in this new face, in this disfigured mask in which no one can see the good, the true, the beautiful, but only their opposites? A tyrant is someone who manipulates, gives orders, enforces discipline, punishes and rewards according to the sovereign and sadistic laws of evil, ugliness, and mendacity. The tyrant: innumerable perfidious travesties, a smug rictus, fastidious and ridiculous uniforms, attacks of hysteria marked by sharp and bestial cries, plaintive infantile whispers, the stamps and roars of boars in rut—or the icy immobility of the vampire.

It isn't hard to believe that the poet-clown has already recognized that face in his nightmares or in the course of his wanderings; it even seems that sometimes, somewhere, he has already borne tyrannical caprice and hatred. No doubt about it, this too is a human face, even when overlaid by wrinkled layers of fat and thick makeup. Yes, yes, the poor man—a vain fanatic, enthralled by the chimera of power, just a poor man, a solitary sufferer who turns his weakness into authority, his fear into assurance, his diseases into violence and farce.

And so, in the bright arena, Auguste the Fool faces the Clown of Power. Their eyes meet. Is all of human tragicomedy concentrated in that brief exchange? Is it attraction by repulsion, a powerful reaction catalyzed by the meeting of opposites? Can they be compared to each other, these actors playing different parts in the coded scenario called *Life on Earth*? Only if one watches the spectacle from the moon, or from so close up that one is blinded and can no longer see the contrasts in this global and rapidly changing masquerade.

An artist who has lived under tyranny (and even one who hasn't) cannot ignore the insurmountable moral barrier that separates the two roles. He can watch the spectacle from a cosmic distance—and yet he is ready to play the part of his opposite to the point of identification with him; he will cross that distance in order to scrutinize the counterpart with all the curiosity, imagination, and precision required by his task. The history of the circus as History? With its strange couple: the Artist-Fool and the Clown of Power?

Is the artist Auguste the Fool, is the tyrant the White Clown? Is Hitler a White Clown, and is Chaplin, who has mimed him with childlike irony, a traditional Auguste the Fool? Is this moment of juncture in the human dynamic the moment of truth in the great circus of the world?

While I am to this day painfully aware of the sinister radiation with which Hitler and Stalin ravaged my childhood and youth, I would never have understood the true nature of this radiation if I hadn't been compelled, in my adult years, to endure—to the point of suffocation—the paranoia of a small provincial tyrant who managed to expand, step by step, the small arena of his macabre circus to cover an entire country.

"Antonioni is a silent Auguste the Fool, mute and melancholic. . . . Picasso? A triumphant Auguste the Fool, proud, confident, a jack-of-all-trades; he emerges victorious in his battle with the White Clown" (Federico Fellini).

In *The Europeans,* Luigi Barzini wrote about his impressions on first meeting Hitler: "To me, then, he looked like an improbable funny burlesque character, a sinister clown. . . . He was, I concluded, too improbable to last; there was nothing to worry about. . . . [He had] no more of a chance than Mussolini's operatic attempt to reconstruct the Roman Empire."

Hitler, a White Clown! And Chaplin, his imitator (or interpreter), is an Auguste the Fool. A buffoon, with a little black hat cocked over his ear, the oversized pants, and the elegant cane of a dandy.

The mask of the White Clown corresponds to the antinomy of good and evil we know from fairy tales and find so satisfying: "The face is white and spectral, with circumflexes above arrogantly raised brows; the mouth a narrow line, hard and unpleasant, distant, cold," says Fellini, "icily authoritarian like certain nuns in charge of kindergartens," but also, above all, "like those spiffy Fascists in shiny black silk and gold braid, riding crop in hand (typical clown gear), giving martial orders."

Is it hard to define the dividing line between Auguste and the White Clown? "There are White Clowns who began as Augustes, but no Auguste the Fool started out as a clown. This is probably the case because it is easier for a tolerant nature to imitate authority than for an authoritarian one to slip into a tolerant character" (Ornella Volta, *Small Encyclopedia of the Clown*).

Our pitiful local clown: his ridiculous, self-awarded, ever more pompous titles, his endless speeches full of vast platitudes with their perennial hoarse bathos, their monotonous invective, their grammatical mistakes. The fear fueling his fanaticism, and the clever camouflage of that fanaticism; his stutter and puppetlike gestures, his manic insistence and schizophrenic industry, and his perplexity when confronted with anything still alive and spontaneous.

Many have started out as Augustes—mediocre housepainters, humble provincial seminarists, apprentices in a cobbler's workshop. "The fascination of the moonstruck, the nocturnal, ghostly elegance" of the White Clown? "To children, the White Clown is a bogeyman because he embodies responsibility or—to use a fashionable term—repression," says Fellini. Repression—a fashionable term? There was a time when I would have responded to that statement with a superior smile, or else with the anguished howl of a sick beast: repression was our tangible present, the air we breathed every day, the atmosphere in every office and restaurant. The children laughed at the tyrant and couldn't understand why all the adults around them let him gain so much power over them. This too is a paradox characteristic of this little clown who differs from Hitler or Stalin in that children find him merely ridiculous.

Ridicule has its own secret power, that of amusement, and it is vengeful. Repeatedly, Fellini refers to the anonymous citizen, "the child who is forced to play the part of Auguste" in his relationship to Mother (the state, the police, the authorities) and her constant prohibitions: "Don't touch that!" "Don't do that!"

By decree, our clown has changed the whole country into a huge kindergarten populated by militarized and industrious children; but he can't stand his own "children," or "subjects." If they obey, he spits on them and beats them up; if they act up, he cuts off an ear; if they disobey, he sews their lips shut; if they get sick, he presents them with a coffin and a bill for funeral expenses. "Order and discipline" are the only virtues he permits the anonymous throng. He communicates with the humble ones—from whose ranks he, the "most beloved, the most honored, the most revolutionary son of the people," has risen—but only through his guards. Anyone who dares intercept the presidential limousine with a petition invariably disappears, never to be seen again. The cape, the scepter, the palace, the anthem, the decorations . . .

And his hunting parties!

The bears tranquilized, foaming at the mouth, bound, prevented from eating and drinking for many days before the hunt begins. The aerial surveillance of the hunting area. The red presidential helicopter landing in front of the castle. The guests from the Party circus, from the circus press, from the foreign embassies. Bit players from the secret police dressed as waiters, and the clown's bodyguards waiting in ditches, camouflaged in the underbrush. The portable fence deployed like a funnel with the opening exactly in front of the president's stand. The tranquilized bears gradually awaken and appear in the arena, unsteady and bellowing. The First Hunter of the Circus taking aim, closing his right eye, then his left. The

moment the comrade places his finger on the trigger, the Securitate
snipers camouflaged in the underbrush also fire, with silencers,
picking off the game. To the rhythm of the national anthem, the
Supreme Clown thrusts out his chest for the gold medal; he is the
best marksman of the time.

And what about his favored black Labrador? Born in England as
Sir Gladstone and renamed, for the circus, Comrade Corbul
(Raven), eating royally, nourished with British dog biscuits sent
weekly by the circus ambassador in London—whose main diplo-
matic task, in fact, this is. The dog enjoys the rank of the highest
officer in the circus hierarchy, but his importance is much greater
than that of any general, admiral, or spymaster in the circus army
and police.[1]

"White Clowns have always competed amongst themselves in
the magnificence of their costumes," says Fellini. There was a very
famous clown, Theodore, who "appeared in a new costume every
day." So does our national clown, but vanity alone does not explain
the tremendous effort this takes: fear plays a part in it. The outfit
for dinner, the outfit for a working visit to the provinces, the one
for important meetings, and the one for secret negotiations—each
and every one of the clown's costumes is a matter of national
importance. A special detachment of the Securitate is responsible
for the clown's daily sartorial and nutritional needs, for a complete
daily change of clothes, from socks and handkerchief to shoes and
headgear. Daily, all this is delivered from a special outfitter's; every
day, a special laboratory analyzes food ingredients and compiles the
perfect menu, while also examining the excretions of the most
beloved's alimentary tract. Special commandos check his office, his
bedroom, his fountain pen, and his toilet for radiation, just in case
some subversive agent, bent on saving the tyrant's subjects, has

---

[1] Although much of the material in the preceding paragraphs was common knowledge in
Romania in the later years of Ceauşescu's regime, the stories did not begin to be published
(as far as I can tell) until after 1989 or 1990. See especially John Sweeney's *The Life and
Evil Times of Nicolae Ceauşescu* (London: Hutchinson, 1991) and István Várhegyi's article
in *Die Zeit* (May 1990).

managed to contaminate a suit, a dish, a chair. At the end of the day, the articles of clothing are stamped with red and green ink (the colors of the Romanian extreme left and right) and taken to be incinerated in the presidential crematorium, which, like the special outfitter and the special laboratory for nutrition and excretion analysis, is part of the gigantic, multifaceted security organization of the great circus.

"The White Clown," says Fellini, "likes to slap people in the face." Our sadistic national clown has proscribed food, light, heat, and travel. He has destroyed churches and archives.

Father, mother, schoolmaster? The White Clown as an embodiment of the Ideal, a knight of Utopia? An implacable visionary of the future, indifferent to the horrors of the transient present, focused only on what *must be done*? Icily authoritarian, like certain nuns in charge of kindergartens?

Some fifteen years ago I made the acquaintance of a doctor who had, in the days when the Communist party was outlawed (1923–44), shared a prison cell with our great clown. I was curious to hear an opinion of him from a man who had been in a position to observe him close up, and daily, as just another cog in the isolated and doom-laden machinery of prison. This was it: "I judged *these people* according to the simplest possible criterion: I tried to imagine what tasks I would give them in my clinic. There was one I might use as an administrator, another who'd do as a driver, cashier, or night watchman. A few could have acquired the skills of a laboratory technician or equipment monitor. But *this one*... no, he couldn't have managed any practical task. He had never done any real work, did not have a craft, would never be able to learn anything. All he could do was make speeches. And boss others around. I couldn't have used him, not even as a night watchman." What the doctor could not explain was why *these people*, as he called his former comrades, now the "new class," were once his soulmates, and why he allowed *this one* to be his political instructor—in such crass disregard of the criterion of normality one would have expected from an intelligent, honest, and courageous physician.

Grade-school children in uniforms with lapel pins. The Pioneer salute. The anthem. The Leader. . . . Families crammed into block housing under the control of a "block guard" installed by the "organs of order and surveillance." Entire city blocks of magnificent villas and one-family houses bulldozed to make room for standardized boxes in which the inhabitants could more efficiently be ordered about and watched. A gigantic program designed to destroy villages in order to transform agriculture into "agri-industrial complexes" and to "eliminate the distinctions between city and country"—to turn farmers into wage slaves, their families boxed into human hives, above, below, and next to each other.

And all women, in both city and country, obliged to submit to regular gynecological examinations to make sure no pregnant woman dares try to deprive the all-owning state of a future subject.

And the old ones sent to special reservations where they have to grow vegetables and clean out stables.

And the extermination of dogs and cats, to ensure the uninterrupted sleep of the "working population."

And in the earpiece of every telephone a tiny electronic cockroach, to enable the state to document and scientifically "care for" its victims.

Order, as much as possible, and the greatest possible degree of discipline. Maximal surveillance (a genuine world record: one fully employed police officer for every fifteen citizens—and, for every police officer, fifteen "volunteer" informers). All this to make sure no undeserving member of the remainder of the populace could fall through the mesh of this gigantic net and divulge some secret of the state: the name of his factory, the measurement of pickle jars, the formula for the atomic bomb, the number of public urinals per city district, the clown's nickname, the holding capacity of the loony bins, the map of the country, the technology for the manufacture of sewing thread. And to make sure that no foreigner could discover the secrets of our paradisiacal circus: avoid all contact with them—this is an honorable duty, and a natural right for those who wish to survive.

Everything has to do with *him*—and his favorite word is *everything*. We shall do everything, everything, *everything*, he barks in a hoarse monotone. To ensure the continuous growth of the leading role . . . the uninterrupted growth of the leading role . . . ever more highly developed discipline . . . and relentless continuous growth of the leading role of the Leader.

Years ago, a friend of mine who'd been living on the outskirts of the city wanted to move to the center. She had found a small apartment for sale on the Calea Victoriei. When it was time to do the paperwork, she found she needed a special permit because her windows faced the street and the Calea Victoriei was one of the main arteries the nation's clown chose for the morning drive to his office in the Central Committee Building, where he would work hard at governing from eight sharp in the morning until eight sharp at night, then return via another artery to the presidential villa. These were sacred streets.

Order, as much order as possible, and vigilance, uninterrupted vigilance, so that nothing could spoil his mood, cause him to become ill, or, above all, bring about the long-anticipated, fatal, liberating accident.

The most valuable resource is the human being, that is: *he.* A specimen like *him,* according to the calculations of the presidential astrologers, occurs only once in five hundred years. This justifies the pains taken over his nutrition, his excretions, his weaponry, the 365 pairs of pants and underpants, socks, pajamas, and nightcaps, the 365 pairs of shoes and slippers.

Then there is the photographer, the barber, the masseur, the cosmetician. There are bodyguards and the stand-ins, and the interpreters for the 364 languages of the globe, of which he doesn't know a single one. The information and disinformation, radiation and counterradiation. The portable toilet, the invisible shower. The noiseless pistol. All in the service of the country's only productive institution: the cult of the clown. And there is, of course, his Pussycat.

"The only female clown to achieve lasting fame is Miss Lulu. Gelsomina and Cabiria in my movies belong to the genus Auguste the Fool. They aren't women, they are sexless," says Fellini. "Charlot, an Auguste, is equally devoid of human gender, just a happy cat that cleans its fur and walks where it pleases." Laurel and Hardy, "two more of the same type, they even sleep together like innocent children, as if sex did not exist. Exactly that was what made the world laugh."

And the Pussycat? The lover with poor teeth, the erudite illiterate, the commissar in skirts, the witch, the hysterical one, Auntie Porno? The spouse of the White Clown: is she, too, a White Clown?

People snicker, not only in secret, about the first couple of the land, forever locked in the presentation of the same routine: *the first couple.* In full regalia, the parvenus stage an imperial intoxication of bliss not seen anywhere outside the circus. He wears a sash and carries a scepter; she dresses in the toga of an empress, conscious of her fame as a scientist, confident of her vaccination certificates. He holds his secret councils with Kojak, Abdullah Jasser, Santiago Carlos, Kim Kung Kang or Benito Mafioso—to discuss the next worldwide measures to be taken for the liquidation of his adversaries and for the conditioning of the survivors to an existence in the catacombs.

Prudish and shy, he airs his obsessions in endless, repetitive, stammering tirades of invective, both at home and at the office. His little Lulu, on the other hand, takes in several sex movies every night, instead of sleeping pills, and falls asleep in a similarly pornographic position, mouth and robe wide open.

Miss Lulu, Lulette, Lena, Leanţa—a vicious White Clown who

dominates her partner and terrorizes his entourage. Out of perversity? Insecurity? Frustration? All of the above, in mutual fidelity; compared to *him*, Hitler was just a waif. "The hermaphrodite" is what they call Hitler, and it is possible to remain a hermaphrodite even though one's spouse has used one to produce children. Hard to imagine our clown in that position, much easier to see her in it—uninhibited, grinning, urging him on, screaming. The most elevated couple: a hermaphrodite and a stale matron . . . Miss Lulena, who walks like a duck, baring her gums above small yellow teeth, mouth open, threads of saliva dripping: and the engorged hermaphrodite, stammering in his red jammies decorated with braid and medals, advancing upon her. Miss Honorary Doctorate, the shameless hussy.

A supreme commander who has never seen combat, a supreme scholar who never finished school. In a golden frame on her ostentatious desk stands *his* portrait, retouched by the best experts of Interpol. On *his* desk, framed in platinum, we see the precious smile of *her* ugliness, decorated with flowerlets and little stars: Miss Lulena, decked out in jewelry and medals and false diplomas, still nothing but a fraudulent Pussycat.

She always spreads her legs, even in the most festive presidential photographs, and always holds her little purse right in front of her pussy, the demotic designation of that unnameable primal spot.

I have taken an infantile, vengeful pleasure in Fellini's text, reading it only from one perspective, reading and rereading it, always with this subtext in mind—to align our ridiculous national clown with all those other White Clowns. Yes, indeed: "the mouth a thin line, cold, full of antipathy, remote" in an ugly face whose homeliness becomes monstrous with its liver spots and its wrinkles born of so much cursing. "Icily authoritarian, like certain nuns in charge of kindergartens"—yes! "Like those spiffy Fascists in shiny black silk and gold braid, riding crop in hand"—yes! A Clown in White in his "striving for higher goals," in his hilarious honky-tonk small-town improvisations, lacking in style and definition, in his sterile, cartoonlike animation à la Duvalier and Idi Amin.

I have exhausted Fellini's text in my secret enjoyment of it; I was incapable of reading it impartially. In a totalitarian state, every detail of everyday life, every word and gesture acquires a distorted and hidden meaning that reveals itself only to the indigenous dwellers. Only those who live in more or less normal societies can find this code lunar and fascinating. That poor, ridiculous creature! An illiterate upstart! Stammerer! Chimpanzee! Monster! Vermin! Leech!

A White Clown? That's too great an honor. . . . He was too small, too unfinished, too stupid for that. Yet it is much harder to see him as belonging to the seemingly more modest, in reality far more distinguished category of Auguste the Fool. That's unthinkable. Auguste is much too dear to me; I have always seen the artist as an Auguste, a loser.

In my last year *there,* I read Montale's great poem "The Poet" countless times. In a time of increasing deterioration and degradation of everyday life, the sovereign sarcasm of his verses helped me at times to endure the ubiquity of the dictator. I knew the poem by heart and repeated it to myself with sadistic determination, carefully measuring out the poison the poet had distilled so masterfully.

"Only a short thread is left me / but I hope I'll be able to dedicate / my humble songs to the next tyrant." Thus Montale begins the confession he ascribes to "a poet." I wasn't alone in sensing that only a short thread was left me: over the years, the tyrant had worn us down, insinuating himself into our daily nightmares, and I knew that even if I managed to save myself, I would be scarred forever by the toxins of this macabre period of my life.

"He will want / spontaneous praise gushing from my grateful / heart and will have it in abundance," I repeated, making faces, thinking of the ghost possessed by this very desire for "spontaneous praise," who lorded it over not only a crowd of poets but also the thousands and again thousands of anonymous frightened people squeezed into his circus prison.

"All the same I shall be able to leave / a lasting trace," I consoled myself, thinking about my famous and not-so-famous predecessors and contemporaries who felt that their only responsibility was to posterity.

The final line, however, I would whisper, since that was the only way I could enjoy the exaltation with which art proclaims its fundamental truth, parodying it at the same time: "In poetry / what matters is not the content / but the form."

That gave me satisfaction. I had already succeeded several times in finding the right form for the encoding of my antipathy for the tyrant; what's more, in my short story "Robot Biography" the aggressive "content" took on a high-risk form when I assigned the twenty-sixth of January as the sinister main character's birthday—the day of tremendous festivities in honor of the tyrant's birth. The horrified reaction of my friends to this impertinent frivolity both delighted and terrified me, but it also gave me hope that other readers would notice how spontaneous aversion had made me demonstrate that form and content are indeed united in works of art.

"Better to be a free human being, never mind all the problems with which one may be burdened, than to be the buffoon of a lamentable buffoon," a friend wrote to me in a letter around the time of the buffoon's birthday. The friend enclosed a big bundle of newspapers that sang the praises of the event. Every year, huge festivities are organized in his honor, with pomp as solemn as it is provincial, making even the policemen laugh as they form the thousand-long human chains to restrain the merriment and pressure of the masses.

For me, this sinister carnival was already a thing of the past; I was on the other side of the wall and had landed in West Berlin, a city that brought to mind similar caricatures and a similar collective brutalization.

I looked at the pile of papers. They seemed to have been printed on toilet paper and tore as soon as you turned a page. The ink left red, green, and black smudges on my fingers. I was barely able to read a few sentences: dementedly repetitive, the clichés chased one another and promptly induced lethal boredom. All the years endured in that empire of horror and perverted language, all the neuroses and nightmares, stirred up the old, indissoluble poison in me.

In those same weeks of painful, intermittent recovery, I came across a repulsive but useful potboiler, a godsend to the Western media's appetite for sensation. Repulsive because of its subject (our little dictator with the speech impediment) and also its author (a former general who had been in charge of the dictator's secret police and now had entered the service of "freedom" and new masters), but useful because of the revelations this connoisseur was offering the public in his depiction of a clan of upstarts, a gang of circus clowns made up of philistines, crooks, and cynics who had gained power and used it to develop their mediocrity and meanness to the fullest degree. There was the trade in Jews and Germans for convertible currencies, euphemistically called "reuniting families"; there was the espionage and disinformation, the hobnobbing with Arab terrorists, fire-eaters, hypnotists, animal tamers from the KGB. There were the situations that made our "Leader" throw up—when, for instance, American authorities wouldn't comply with his demand for an "official" ban on protest demonstrations during his visit to New York, or when he heard that he'd been betrayed by one of his most faithful servants; the attack of hysteria when he first met the new U.S. ambassador, who was black (an insufferable insult to an old internationalist). I read about the tantrums of his spouse, the one with many honorary degrees, directed against their circus house managers when they had forgotten to place orders for special toilet bowls from Paris or London. I found out about her piquant "hobby" of watching movies of adulteries committed by some of the highest figures of the state, clandestinely filmed by Securitate specialists for this express purpose.

It probably was no accident that during this same period between Inferno and Purgatory (tyranny and exile) I found, in a Parisian journal, these sentences addressed to Julien Hervier by Ernst Jünger: "The artist has to focus on his painting, his poetry, his sculpture, the rest is ridiculous. That is why I could never criticize an artist who benefits from the favors of a tyrant. He can't say: 'I'll wait until the tyrant is overthrown!' because that might take ten years, and in the meantime his creative power would wane."

I agreed that "the rest is ridiculous." It is, however, not just a question of the ridiculous but also, first and foremost, of the horror, the destruction of the last enclaves of quotidian normality, the daily risk of physical and spiritual death. It was impossible to escape from that "rest," which had become the all-encompassing, aggressive, absurd, and suffocating *whole.*

The buffoon of a lamentable buffoon? To the best of my ability, I managed to sidestep the monster's masks and traps. I never vied for the tyrant's favors, I wouldn't have granted him a syllable of praise. Dead-eyed, I stared at the dead pages of the dead newspapers. Suddenly, Fellini's "impertinent loudspeaker" came to mind: "A loudspeaker, an Auguste, simply refuses to transmit the program given by a White Clown."

All the dishonest newspapers that poisoned our days with their unchanging refrain, all the loudspeakers playing the same tune: what if, one day, they provoked a revolt, what if they found a method of revenge, of mockery, by changing, reversing the code? A warped sentence, a missing letter that simply escapes from one of his great honorary titles, an impertinent blot on the idyllic retouched photograph. . . . At the right moment, the "impertinent loudspeaker" manages to pull off a gag that serves to demean the tyrant: "It surrounds him, ridicules him, mocks everything the White Clown utters," says Fellini. "It is the revolt of the means of communication—roars and altered news to counter the insulting nonsense loudspeakers were forced to disseminate during the Fascist years." And not only during those: our generation had its own White Clowns and everyone was his Auguste.

I refused to serve our tyrannical clown not because I disdained his favors but because I tried to ignore him as best I could. I wasn't even interested in that realm of the "ridiculous" that can only be called "the rest" of the very first shaky and confused days of terror that later mounted rapidly and murderously, like an avalanche that collects, devours, annihilates everything in its path. I took good care not to hate him, because that would have meant granting him too much importance—even though like a huge, tireless octopus he had already discharged so much shit that we were almost suffocating under it. Now that everybody hated him and hoped for his death, there was no longer anything one could do against him.

Only when a disaster has become obvious and irreversible does hatred become irreversible: against Hitler, only in the final months of the war, when disaster overwhelmed the entire German people; against Stalin only after his death, when the monster was no longer dangerous and the myth had turned rancid.

All the heads of state of both East and West received our ridiculous national monster with highest honors. Even during his first period in power, while he was still exploiting misconceptions and presented himself as a champion of the good, he disgusted me just as much as in his final decade. I was instinctively suspicious and disdainful of him even before he started baring his teeth in the horrendous Grand Guignol performance. It would not have been possible for me to dismiss the entire masquerade as only the "ridiculous rest." With increasing frequency, he unsheathed his claws, and his bark grew ever louder. His demonic, murderous ridiculousness was no negligible "rest," it was the *whole,* and no one was able to escape.

*   *   *

Not long after the tyrant came to power, a writer who moved in medical circles showed me a "psychiatric profile" of the tyrant prepared by a group of respected specialists. Even then there was reason to fear the worst: even then, this leader, this best-beloved son of the people, should have been taken into custody without delay, on grounds provided by these documents.

Soon his paranoia became evident: in labor legislation that tied every wage earner to his place of employment, to force obedience and facilitate surveillance; in family legislation that made divorce difficult to obtain, banned abortion, and discriminated against unmarried couples; in school legislation aimed at the politicization and militarization of children. It was obvious in his tirades, delivered in a state of trance for hours on end to starving audiences, about the future of the circus to be built by happy slaves whipped ever onward by stern kindergarten teachers. The clown kept in his circus troupe only the hypnotized dwarves whose job it was to applaud him, and the brawny armored giants who made up his national security system.

Even back then, I was cautiously preparing my departure from the "labor zone," as it was called in the language of the menagerie, a zone that was to become, in less than a decade, a swamp for rhinos to wallow in, those who like to bathe in ordure and denounce others.

One needn't exert one's imagination too much to visualize the state of revulsion and fear, exhaustion and depression, that drives a person to the psychiatrist. The latter knows, of course, that the illness in question is affecting all of society, but each patient is an individual case whose "self-denunciation" has to be taken seriously and treated.

It is a razor's-edge situation in which Auguste the Fool no longer just mimes ambiguity but is possessed by it, and in which the boundary between hallucination and reality begins to dissolve. A minute dose of "simulation"—for example, the assignment of excessive importance to certain real symptoms (or others derived from one's reading)—can ultimately lead to a genuine disturbance.

In the totalitarian circus, where faking is not immediately obvious to either the physician or the less aware patient, the waiting rooms of psychiatrists' offices become sanctuaries of refuge, prayer, simulation. They become "legal" hiding places where one can withdraw from the marshy arena and its lies, punishments, and daily moans.

Since psychiatric repression has been used against so many "undesirables," it may seem unconscionable to hand the state the simplest weapon it can use to destroy you. And I didn't belong to the "desirable" ones, then or later. And yet . . . My patient waiting in front of physicians' offices did finally lead to "liberation" and "victory": I was declared unfit to work. The annual humiliation of a medical examination protected me from a multitude of other daily humiliations. Had the truly diseased one (who'd made the entire nation ill) decided to retire, be it for obvious "reasons of health" or for reasons of age—equally obvious for a long time—I would have "recovered." As things were, I was the afflicted one, and the portrait of the buffoon that stared at me from every street corner compelled me to increase daily the dosage of my medication. Thus, at last, a connection had been established between us. The curious role reversal was just a pale reflection of the schizophrenia the true madman had imposed on his entire domain.

In such borderline situations, what becomes quite evident is the fundamental difference between the interpretation of a role—with its subtle symptom common to all professional diseases, including the play called life and the play called death—and the actual role a human being has been assigned on the great stage of the world.

Does the White Clown represent only ridiculous authority, and Auguste contrariness, laughter, and suffering? "The appearance of a White Clown (the Fascist) transforms us into similar clowns as soon as we surrender and return the Roman salute in a disciplined fashion," says Fellini.

"You are much too serious. You are too ethical, and you are not playful enough. The image of Auguste the Fool doesn't fit you at all," said a friend years ago after I published *Auguste the Fool's Apprenticeship Years.* Suffering to the point of grimaces, I was forced to accept Auguste the Fool as an autobiographical reality. This identification was not only a result of a withdrawal from my surroundings, of loneliness and its burden of vulnerability, and it was also more than a simple refusal to obey; it was in fact a consequence of my deep solidarity with people's unhappiness.

The bad actor gradually polarized the hatred of a whole shackled nation into lethargy and despair. In this state of tragic, general despair, Auguste's laughter and tears gain a great resonance among his fellow sufferers.

Existence under terror distorts your perceptions and frequently tempts you to make risky and farfetched associations. No matter how far you have removed yourself from that existence in both time and space, it is impossible to rid yourself of your dark obsessions.

In the summer of 1988, in Washington, I watched the circus of the presidential elections and was reminded of the clown "back there." The presidency of the Actor was over, and now it was time for the new actors of the new presidency. The childish and vulgar theater of competition for acclamation gave rise, in the exiled Auguste, to rather pessimistic thoughts about the human species. Anyone coming from the so-called socialist East needs some time to rid himself of illusions about the "reverse" Utopia. But even if these disappointments were irritating and if the new Vice President Coturnix reminded me—surprisingly enough—less of telegenic Robert Redford than of a minor Stalinist party secretary in a provincial town of the fifties, my terror still remained *over there.*

Only over there could my reading of Fellini's essay evoke that childlike *Schadenfreude* in me. Even if one watches the American election circus on the tube through Fellini's telescopic lens, one is still *over there* in one's mind. This may be so because Jünger's statement applies *only* to old or young democracies in which one still has the option to ignore the political brouhaha, or at least to put it in parentheses. That, however, becomes impossible when the ridiculous reigns supreme over all of human life, tortures everyone without respite, and slowly but surely cripples them: then it is not only *the rest* that is ridiculous, but the whole, and it can't be ignored because it won't ignore you, won't let you go.

The circus of free, freely manipulated elections in a democratic society does not give cause for optimism. While watching it I was spontaneously reminded of the FBI file on Charlie Chaplin, discovered years after his death. It was nineteen hundred pages long, covering the period between 1922 and 1978 (thus extending one whole year beyond his demise), and contained so many absurdities that no satirical cabaret could do them justice. And yet, while witnessing all the shallow gags that accompanied the spectacle of the U.S. presidential elections, all I could think about was the incomparable face of our tiny national clown.

Are the tyrant and the suppressed masses truly irreconcilable in every respect, or is it a matter of unconscious reciprocal stimulation? Do labor camps and totalitarianism arise only when a society's energy is perverted and suffocated? Is the dictator only the enemy or also the creation of the masses?

"It is said that Antonet, a famous White Clown, never spoke a word to Beby, his Auguste, outside the arena," Fellini writes. The clown takes revenge on the anonymous masses from whence he comes and throws tantrums when his superiority is not admired. How did our national clown react to the modest love affairs of his daughter? Or (how shameful!) to the marriage of his son—to a Jewish woman! No one even bothered to explain the national

importance of the new divorce laws to that imprudent boy; they
simply mailed the divorce decree to him.

Could it be that the dictator too is an artist, obsessed with the
impossible? Could we consider the diseased, fanatical boy who
called himself Caligula a poet just because he appointed his favorite
horse to a ministerial post? Does the gigantically morbid ever
achieve the ineffable distant horizon all poetry strives toward? Is the
despot a knight of Utopia?

Duality inheres in every human being, certainly in poets and also
in leaders, even though the latter like to forget it. "The stationmas-
ter in my movie was a White Clown, and thus all of us become
Augustes. When you stand in front of a White Clown, you can't
help but assume the role of Auguste," confesses Fellini, who then
adds: "But only the appearance of an even more sinister clown, the
Fascist, transformed us into White Clowns when he forced us to
return the Roman salute in a disciplined fashion."

Finally, the author attempts to define his own location in the
fabulous circus of the world. "If I try to imagine myself as a clown,
I end up seeing myself as Auguste the Fool." In the real world it
seems risky to venture between the uncertain and diffuse bound-
aries that define human experience. "Yes, I consider myself an
Auguste the Fool, but I am also a White Clown," Fellini continues.
Then he concludes with a meditative sentence: "But perhaps I am
the director of the circus, the physician of the mad who has himself
become mad." An outsider, a pariah, a melancholy dreamer and an
unwavering researcher, an undecided mime, a man obsessed by
irresolvable questions.

Does the chimera of reality become more real than reality itself?
Among the characters whose passions and follies the artist lives
through, whose disasters he "appropriates" and whose abysses he
illuminates, he must not forget that of the tyrant. We encounter the
tyrant among children, not only among despotic kindergarten

teachers, among married couples and lovers, parents, grandparents, co-workers, and recruits. Only too often, he sits on the highest throne and terrorizes a whole nation, a whole world. He lives his part without being aware of it; he is simply an aberration of nature. Paradoxically or not, only art can render this horrifying, real, cyclical natural catastrophe credible and mysterious. (Alfred Jarry's words on his deathbed reveal the identification that can exist between an author and his creation: "Daddy Ubu will now try to sleep.")

The minor comedian, the paranoid hero, who has fulfilled his ambition to take over the world's great stage for a while with his attacks of arrogance, devastating masquerades, absurd rituals—it is possible that even he, the tyrant, is granted moments of fanatical insight, but he will never be blessed with the clarity and talent of the artist who interprets him for a while. Chaplin plays Hitler with the same degree of genius that he applied to so many other, different, even diametrically opposed roles, whereas Hitler only "played" himself.

Does unwavering observation of the grotesqueness and vanity of power finally lead one to a kind of compassion tinged with fear, or to an arrogant feeling of purity and superiority?

During my final year *over there* I saw him at close range. Not on television, greeted with somersaults and magic tricks by some presidential colleague at some foreign circus, nor on a trip within the country on the occasion of one of those "working visits" that begin with the howling and twitching of the masses, continue with his advice bestowed on trained slaves in factories, stables, colleges, crematoria, schools for parrots, and end with an endless speech on hair-raising visions of the future, the same speech delivered a thousand times before, always in front of the same horrified captive audience.

No, this time I experienced him in tangible proximity. I had just returned from the police precinct where I had submitted my typewriter to its obligatory annual examination: in the national clown's opinion, only those worthy of a special permit were entitled to the possession of such an instrument. To obtain this special permit, one had to fill out a form and pass an annual test that involved a personal appearance, dangerous machine in hand, at the police precinct of one's residence, to have the form checked and also to type a control text just in case a letter had changed, an exclamation point or a comma had worn out, or—even worse—in case the owner and hence the machine had been stricken with some contagious disease that could be transmitted through typed pages, causing a collective epidemic. As everyone knows, the viruses of our time are such sly and stubborn creatures, well camouflaged, almost invisible, but aggressive, terribly aggressive, and simply unstoppable once they get going.

I had to wait my turn for over an hour, but everything went without a hitch. There were a lot of people waiting in front of room 23, the number indicated on my form. Particularly impressive were the old folks struggling in with their heavy old models. The three young officials in civilian garb, probably members of the Securitate, were polite and bored, possibly even mildly skeptical about the value of this new circus routine; in any case, the procedure was performed with dispatch.

First came the routine questions. Do you own an automobile? If so, what make? Do you own your apartment or do you live in a state-owned apartment? Who shares it with you? Employment of spouse? Relatives abroad? Trips abroad? Relatives in this country? Any members of the Party Central Committee or employees of the Ministry of the Interior? I knew that the questions had to be answered in writing in one's own hand. They no longer shocked me as they had the first time, when their absurdity and utter irrelevance to the subject of this test still had an intimidating effect. I filled out the form in a quick scrawl, then typed two copies of the assigned text, as well as two sets of the impressions made by every key, and received, once again, my permit. Feeling quite good about it all, I headed back home with my magical toy.

While still in the elevator, I heard the piercing, paralyzing howl of a police siren. The militia! I hurried to unlock the door to my small apartment and ran to the balcony. The siren didn't stop, it was announcing an event: a small motorcade consisting of his limousine, then the limousine of his favorite dog, the ever-present huge black Labrador, the emergency physician's car, three police cars, and finally three less conspicuous vehicles carrying "technical" personnel. Indeed, a modest convoy compared with his entourage on other working visits. This was obviously one of those unannounced blitz visits that the nation's clown decided upon as if struck by electricity, to the dismay of his unprepared subjects. Undoubtedly a surprise visit, because otherwise the sidewalks would have been packed with a dense crowd of applauding citizens, women, children, soldiers, employees, transported here for that express purpose.

The national clown wished to inspect the progress of construction of the White Palace. He had ordered the razing of some of the prettiest quarters of the city to make room for the palace and the Circus Boulevard that cut the city in two—or nine, or however many—segments, so that the Great Presidential Circus would finally dominate the skyline.

The convoy came to a halt next to the small bridge across the stinking waters of the city canal. He wanted to view the Perspectives of the Future. Around him swirled a gaggle of subordinates waving and carrying plans, maps, and portfolios, anxiously eager to anticipate the direction of his next step and to decipher the meaning of his every gesture with due alacrity. These were elegantly attired gentlemen, construction engineers, sculptors, decorators with crazed purple faces, jerking about in a frenetic Saint Vitus' dance, stumbling and stammering.

The surrounding balconies filled with gawkers: office workers, housewives, children. This was not the command audience that would obey police instructions to congregate at predestined points along the clown's route. For a moment one couldn't know what to expect from this mass of people; then some began to . . . applaud.

Not to yell, not to complain or curse—no, applause it was, even though sporadic, a sleepy reflex, an automatic reaction to a ritual that had entered their bloodstreams ever since the first circus routines to which they had been driven under the lash of severe kindergarten teachers. It was conventional applause but nevertheless spontaneous, independent of the usual pressure exerted by the police, perhaps triggered by fear of colleagues and neighbors.

I saw him plainly: from the 365 sets of his annual wardrobe, the special outfitters had chosen the appropriate one—overalls tailored from buff-colored silk. A rumpled cockney cap had been planted on his head, pulled down close to his eyebrows. His movements were deliberate, he did not raise his voice but seemed calm and sensible, not unlike a modest shopkeeper, and took notes on what people told him on a small pad. Everyone in his entourage took notes as well. The little boss seemed to pay special attention to everything the spiffy specialists managed to tell him, paralyzed by fear as they were. According to the day's predetermined program, he listened to them in silence. Among all these confused people he looked like the only normal person, the only one who could afford the mask of normality. The hysterically obsequious behavior of the cast of eminent authorities and the clown's slightly weary jester's calm established the beat of this touching and horrifying contredance.

The observer's confusion lasts only a moment: then he becomes aware of the fact that this comedian has destroyed his life, poisoned his days, his and everybody else's—this pitiful windblown vagabond, this gutter demagogue! His white mask—white as his skull. Is it a feeling of humiliation to have lived so many years terrorized by a caricature—or is it grief over the human species in general?

For a moment, the observer feels unapproachably superior to this wild charade, suddenly transfigured by such crystalline incongruity—thus, an aristocrat: he, the outcast, the "artist," already knows that he'll have to pitch his tent elsewhere, as far as possible from this blood-drenched arena. ("He can't say: 'I'll wait until the tyrant is overthrown!' because that might take ten years, and in the meantime his creative power would wane.")

This last confrontation lasts only a second. Then he shakes the weariness off his shoulders, out of his head and his entire body, as if wanting to rid himself of the poison that has invaded his every fiber.

Irreversible time, time that gives nothing back: neither the house nor the books, neither the abandoned projects nor the lost friends.

Is it possible for evil to really be embodied by such pitiful and ridiculous envoys? Does the grandiose imprint of hell manifest itself in these laughable (even if terrible) stammered pantomimes?

He isn't even worth a curse. Nothing and No One and Nowhere—this is the summation of this catastrophe, concrete and terrible as it was.

His caricature grins from every wall of the country, the country that once embodied hope. A hope of a life, for better or worse, but a life: in the light of youth, at the time of decline, in the intoxication of love, in rebellious dreams as well as bitter disappointment. For better or worse? It was never free in any case, but it became hell only after the skeleton of this plague rose up against the firelit sky, in this carnival that glorified the future and celebrated death. He is tiny and white, the clown, a little white mouse, a carrier of the plague: a death's-head of nothingness.

Life *back there* consisted of waiting, of permanent preparation for something uncertain and continually postponed. That was the life this Auguste the Fool led until yesterday. A life in permanent suspension. Now it lies behind him, ever farther behind him, and yet it has stayed with him like a wound that won't heal, it partakes of every step he takes. A quote from the teachings of Rabbi Moshe Loeb: "The road through this life is like a razor's edge: hell on one side, hell on the other. Between those two runs the road through life."

What awaits this wanderer, a somersault into the void? the senselessness of new masquerades? the vulnerable postadolescence of the aimless stranger among strangers? And what about big words, dear to children and old people and cherished by poets: freedom, conscience, dignity, bravery, sacrifice? They will do for the embellishment of gravestones.

"The loneliness of the poet—what is the loneliness of the poet?" This was a question in a questionnaire that a group of writers fond of aphorisms and wordplay amused themselves with in the first postwar years.

"A circus routine that hasn't been announced." That was the answer given by the young poet Paul Celan before he went into exile in the West, forty years ago.

Bard College
Summer 1989
Translated by Anselm Hollo

CENSOR'S REPORT

With Explanatory Notes by the Censored Author

"Freedom is a more complex and delicate thing than force," wrote Thomas Mann.[1]

Certainly more delicate. But is force, with all its pathological implications, such a simple and direct mechanism? Should the rapid collapse of Communist power in Eastern Europe in 1989 be taken as a conclusive argument that the colossus was simplistic and precarious, made of clay and easily destroyed?

That would be to forget too quickly the muddled, subterranean corridors of the totalitarian system—and we must not forget that there are dark corners where force or power can be found, even in the complex and delicate world of freedom.

The Securitate's secret tunnels, revealed to the whole world during the fighting in Bucharest, provide a spectacular "visualization" of the system of terror, duplicity, and corruption by which tyranny branched out throughout all levels of the population; this intimidation apparatus was incomparably more complex and sinister than that represented by the bands of fanatics seen during the uprising ready to fight to the death by any means necessary to save their skins. In a country with approximately four million (opportunist) members of the party of power, and with a vast

---

[1] Mann to Erika and Klaus Mann, December 1938. *Letters of Thomas Mann, 1889–1955*, Richard and Clara Winston, ed. and trans. (New York: Alfred A. Knopf, 1971), p. 290.

network of informers in all institutions (even in apartment build-
ings), it would be hard to believe that the struggle that took place
in Romania at the end of 1989 was—as the press claimed—simply between the Securitate on one hand and the army and the
people on the other. We need only recall that the number of
Securitate members in the army and among the people was enormous. . . . The weapons of power were not only those that could
be seen and heard, in that terrible confrontation for freedom, but
many others besides: more numerous, more subtle, and even more
cruel, if we consider that the less visible weapons—driven deep
into the society's mentality—have a far longer-lasting effect. It
will be much harder to recover from the lengthy and labyrinthine
process of degradation imposed by those recently in power than
to solve the numerous administrative, economic, and material
problems on the complex and delicate path to democracy and
freedom.

Censorship—the secret police of the word—was for over forty
years one of the most redoubtable weapons of power. Censors are
often perceived as merely narrow-minded bureaucrats. They often
were. But "multilaterally developed"[2] socialism refined the institution of power and increasingly employed well-educated, cynical,
intelligent people in these positions. The methods used by the
institution also evolved and with time became more "complex,"
more "delicate." In short, more perfidious.

At the end of the seventies censorship was "abolished" in Romania. The dictator himself came up with the idea that the ambiguity that had been so "successful" in his foreign policy should be
multilaterally developed at home as well, to fend off the still-timid
objections in the foreign press to his repression.

Romania's anti-Soviet position was used as proof of so-called
independence but it was also an excuse to consolidate a Byzantine
nationalist-socialist state that took lessons in tyranny from all
sources regardless of geography, history, or ideology. It main-

---

[2] A favorite and much-overused phrase of Ceauşescu's.

tained friendly relations with Israel and very close ones with Arab terrorists as well. The "free emigration" policy served the old nationalist dream of "purifying" the population and at the same time brought in hard currency, as Israel and the Federal Republic of Germany paid for each freed citizen; meanwhile the policy gained Romania points with the U.S. Congress. This ambiguity in foreign policy won the dictatorship a stupefying sympathy in the West, as seen in Charles de Gaulle's courtesy gestures, in the paeans by Gerald R. Ford and Richard M. Nixon to the "freedom" in Romania, in the high-level hospitality offered the tyrant at the courts of England and Sweden, or in the frequent visits and encouragement from West German dignitaries, among many other examples. Whether the result of naïveté or cynicism, all this contributed unforgivably to intimidating any attempt at opposition within the country.

The moment had come for Romanian public opinion, feeble, easily manipulated, and without foreign support, to be humiliated and smothered once and for all by the Leader's "genius." An original Romanian synthesis of nazism and Stalinism, with the addition of a few fashionable artificial ingredients, was to be created under the name of a "new democracy."

A series of contradictory actions was undertaken all at the same time: on the one hand the apparatus of surveillance and repression was strengthened, while on the other, some seemingly more democratic forms of government were established, the main purpose of which was to redirect public dissatisfaction away from the Communist party and Securitate and toward the local administrations (which of course were run strictly from above) or toward coworkers and neighbors, the drivers of the overcrowded buses, the clerks in the bare shops, and so on—a kind of substitution of cause for effect that produced, in the short run, results acceptable to the power.[3]

---

[3] In "The End of Communism in Poland and Hungary" (*New York Review of Books,* June 15, 1989, p.6), Timothy Garton Ash used "the power" in this same sense in writing about

The concept of "substitution" became widespread, not only as a deceitful political tactic but in domestic areas like food and clothing: genuine products were gradually replaced by substitutes, not just of incomparably lower quality but often simply by fakes. The same happened in cultural matters; a number of very "outspoken" members of the upper echelons of the official writers were permitted to criticize some negative aspects of the society, aspects that were taboo to others. At the same time they attacked honest intellectuals and artists in order to marginalize and isolate them. This manipulation of opinion—approved by the Power—provided a diversion, a short breather for the public. And yet it was another sham: the "criticism," no matter how harsh (and it was often very primitive, perfectly resembling the object-subject criticized), was automatically "dialectical" and invariably concluded with an affirmation of complete loyalty to the Leader and his state and ideology. All employees had to pay "special" taxes; a monthly percentage of their paychecks was held back to make them "co-owners" of various failed businesses. The workers are the producers, beneficiaries, and proprietors of all goods, said the Leader with his unfailing common sense.

The "new democracy" developed ever-new strategies of substitution. Enormous congresses of workers (industrial, agricultural, educational, and cultural) were periodically convened to approve of the Leader's "precious directions" for the next stage in the country's disastrous development along the shining road to communism. There was an intent to involve everyone in this complicity so that blame was shared by all in varying degrees. Every official act had at least two aspects, if not more: on the one hand there was a cynical show of a demagogic, grotesque "new democracy," while on the other, ever newer and more refined methods were found to mislead and crush the citizen. Duplicity became the disease of the entire country, both at the Party apparatus level and at the level of the

---

Poland: "Almost no one imagined that the great gulf between 'the power' and 'the society,' between Jaruzelski and Walesa, could be swiftly bridged."

masses, who used it for survival. The guilt was general but there were many levels. Some were guilty, while others had guilt imposed upon them.

In order to apply for permission to go abroad it became necessary to obtain the workers' approval first: that is, to get a recommendation from a committee of co-workers who in turn were told by a Securitate officer (one was installed in every institution) what response the applicant should receive from his colleagues.

As the new nationalist-socialist regime sought a legitimacy that could only be ambiguous, it used a new rhetoric that combined old Stalinist slogans and extreme right-wing slogans with an elastic language perceived as more palatable to the West.

A new generation of apparatchiks had by now arisen, young university graduates who had doctorates and had even studied abroad in some cases; their cynicism began to show results. The Party sometimes succeeded in "replacing" real intellectuals (who had become increasingly isolated, worn down, and terrorized) with this substitute class from the privileged "elite." These intellectual substitutes were even allowed to level "charges" against some negative aspects of the society. All kinds of novels and poems were published, in very large editions, that "unmasked" abuses from past or more recent times, signed by official authors, well paid and two-faced. The manipulation of these "charges" by the system was a basic premise of the "dialectical" and vigorous "debate" that the Power encouraged (as when a defense lawyer reiterates the arguments of the prosecution in order to turn the words around and twist their meaning in his own favor).

The success of these "substitutes" was ensured by the public's craving for any kind of bread, meat, books, clothing, entertainment, or information, no matter how fake: there was nothing else, and even these substitutes were available only rarely, at the whim of the ruling family.

At the end of the seventies a presidential decree abolished the Department of the Press (the censor), one of the few efficient institutions in the system. The Party was sure that, after more than

three decades of totalitarian rule, self-censorship and mutual surveillance could brilliantly replace the professionals.

The work of this office was to be taken on, naturally, by—"the
workers." In practice of course, as before, not so much as an
obituary or advertisement could be printed without the approval of
the workers' appointed substitutes. Newspapers, publishers, journals, printers had to arrange for censorship through "specialized"
internal councils.

But self-censorship, which had been exercised successfully for
decades, now no longer fulfilled the expectations of the Party
bureaucracy. So great was the thirst for truth, so far-reaching and so
diverse the intrigues (not only for ill but sometimes for good as well),
that the number of texts disturbing to the authorities steadily grew.

Corrective measures soon followed. Under the Council for Socialist Culture and Education—and its new Reading Service—
censorship was "strengthened" by a great variety of intermediary
measures. Censorship doubled, tripled, diversified, while the
"purification" of texts took on new and ever more duplicitous
methods. Skeptics even held that the motive behind the "abolition"
of censorship was the Power's desire to cause strong dissatisfaction,
so that authors unhappy with the new "democratic" system would
beg (through "charges," petitions, and other democratic means) for
a return to the old central institution with its clear objectives and
logical methods. Indeed, the growing tensions of daily life under
catastrophic economic conditions were inevitably reflected in increasingly exasperated texts.

This then was the situation in Romania during the years when
I was writing my novel *The Black Envelope.* I had posted a quote
from Thomas Mann on the wall in front of my desk: "The novel,
because of its analytical spirit, its consciousness, its innate critical
attitude, is forced to flee social and political conditions in which
poetry may continue to flower quietly on the fringes, undisturbed
and sweetly oblivious of the world."[4] Mann wrote these words

---

[4] Mann to Eduard Korrodi, February 3, 1936, *Letters,* p. 247.

during a period of Nazi frenzy, when the Führer's politicians claimed that only prose writers, not the poets (bearers of the "high German spirit"), had chosen to emigrate. My selection of this quote was not mere chance.

As I wrote I was struggling with the impossible around and within myself. Every day I resolved to stop writing. "My moral-critical conscience is in a state of constant exacerbation, and it is becoming more and more impossible for me to continue pursuing the, it may be, sublime game of novel writing until I have 'rendered an accounting' and unburdened my heart of its concern, its perceptions, its pain, as well as of its freight of hatred and contempt,"[5] wrote Mann during the dark years of horror. My "game," played out in a time and place of horror, was unfortunately inseparable from this great need to ease my burden, which was unbearable and yet—bizarrely enough—stimulating in the resistance it engendered. And yet I wrote! A single obsession focused my worries: that my book should not be co-opted by the system!

It was not by chance that I placed at the center of my novel the Deaf-Mute Association, organized according to "the principles of democratic centralism" and in the spirit of the Party. Was this a "socialist" version of the underground organization of the blind in Ernesto Sábato's novel *On Heroes and Tombs*? That and more.

It was an attempt to find a metaphor for our blocked and handicapped society, for the unrelieved inner pressure and suffering, for the gloomy frustration. And to create another reality, to express ours: endless lines (for bread, gloves, soap, gasoline, toilet paper), apocalyptic hospitals, ubiquitous informers, bombastic charade; the cold and the fears and the jokes and indifference and exhaustion and terror and even my own agonies. Individual man and the masses. Despair, love, fear, guilt, weakness, dreams, and nightmares.

In the spring of 1985 I feverishly put together *The Black Envelope* from hundreds of agonized pages, because my book was included

---

[5] Mann to Karl Kerényi, August 4, 1934, *Letters*, p. 247.

on the state publishing plan for that year: I thought I'd better try while I had the opportunity.

By the end of November the publishers had still received no reply from the Reading Service of the Council for Socialist Culture and Education. The answer came in December. I could tell from the embarrassment of the editors that it was not favorable. I was not given access to the censor's report. For over three decades these reports were considered state secrets. Now that censorship had been "abolished," they had become an even more secret secret. Censor's report? The reports of the new censor's office were not even signed; I found out that they were simply marked with the readers' I.D. numbers—for use by their superiors, of course. The reports were carefully stored in the Archives of the Truth. The results of the reports were transmitted (orally, I presume) to the director of the publishing house, never to the author, who was thus unable to hold a dialogue with the (nonexistent) institution or the (invisible) censor.

I finally received the galleys marked out with discreet checks on the offending portions and pages, about 80 percent of the text. I tried to decode the censor's objections. There were clearly far too many; it seemed impossible to change the text to such a degree. The inadmissible ranged from individual words ("food lines," "informer," "meat," "cold," "coffee," "breasts," "God," "anti-Semitism," "dictator," "dark," "homosexual") to sentences to whole chapters. I gave up: I did not see how one could fight such a thorough and hostile censor. The book sat for a long time without the author or the publisher doing anything about it.

Now I began to feel the side effects of having written a banned book. Excerpts from the novel, already accepted for publication by various literary journals, were withdrawn at the last moment. Articles about the author were cut as well. The press began to avoid my increasingly suspect name.

I read through the galleys again. I "corrected" words and sentences. Here and there I replaced a passage. Useless! Sent "up," the manuscript was returned untouched to the editor and author. I was given to believe that the censor considered my "improvements" trivial and hypocritical.

At an impasse like this an author must make a difficult decision: to go on stubbornly fighting, step by step, conceding as little as possible but accepting compromises to get the book published, or to give up.

Giving up presupposes a kind of hope: a hope for political change, or for publication abroad, or for publication in posterity. In 1985–86 the only hope for a political thaw was the "biological solution": the long-awaited and long-delayed death of the Leader. And what chance was there of sending a manuscript abroad when contact with foreigners was illegal and surveillance was absolute? And who would publish a long, cryptic novel from a virtually unknown literature? As for posterity, that is not only an unknown quantity but paradoxically also "state property." You can never be certain that you have found a perfect hiding place for a manuscript about which the censor's office (and its assistants in the Securitate) knows too much. Some Romanians even believed that all the "true literature" of this dark period was lying in Securitate safes. Certainly it will be compulsory for historians of this time of horror (called, in the official press, "the years of enlightenment") to look in the immense, secret state library for confiscated manuscripts— that is, in the closets and safes and cellars of the Securitate's Superior Council.

In early 1986 my publisher took the first step toward finding a possible solution, by the same method used by the power against his subjects and his own institutions: substitution.

This publisher was among the few who, under the circumstances of absolute terror and in spite of the pressure exerted by censorship, tried to publish good books that were discomforting to the Power. The editors, themselves well-known authors, persevered in a kind of desperate though increasingly exhausted intellectual resistance.

I will not easily forget the morning in January 1986 when I accompanied the director of the publishing house to a florist. He carried the flowerpot to the building of someone whose help he had, after much hesitation, decided to seek. One last step that might save the book and help the author. This was a person of experience and authority in the realm of censorship who would still play the role of "outside" reader (consultant). Thus the publisher was looking for a *substitute* reviewer specializing in the obscure area of censorship. Former censors—these were common enough—with enough intelligence and prestige to sign a regular reader's report with modifications acceptable to the censor's office, but without officially involving the (nonexistent) censor's office. The substitute report, signed by this individual, could be shown to the author. This seemed a real possibility for getting out of the impasse. (The function of this professional underscores better than anything else the duplicity of the system. The report offered tricks and the necessary rhetoric to the author so that both author and censor could work out a strategy of complicity to publish the book.)

In March 1986 I received a "working copy" of the substitute report. I read it in great excitement. I had never seen a censor's report before, only the results—sentences and whole chapters had been cut from my manuscripts and from articles about my work. It had even happened with a book already in print. Distribution was held up and the volume "restructured" by the last-minute removal of some of the stories.

The substitute report gave me an idea of how the "original" indictment in the Archives of the Truth must look. The "literary" form neither surprised nor reassured me. I was sure that the earlier censor had written even more subtly.

I was scared. Yes, just plain scared! Those lines in my novel in which the similarities between nazism and the current Romanian dictatorship were implied had been "deciphered"—yes, scared. I had the feeling that at any moment the door might open and I might be arrested on the basis of this *substitute.* And I imagined how my files would have looked in the Archives of the Truth!

And this was a report intended to help me. Duplicity was the avenue. The author's duplicity, the reader's duplicity? The editor's duplicity, even the censor's and the substitute's duplicity? Duplicity as a social code for communication in daily life, even in the creative life. The author who writes under a totalitarian regime would like the artifices, allusions, codes, and the raw images, direct and brutal, put into the writing to reach the reader to whom they are addressed in a kind of sad, implicit solidarity, and at the same time he hopes to be ignored by the censor. It is at this point that this inevitable duplicity weighs heavily on the captive writer.

Hard days and nights, filled with doubt, fear, and disgust in the struggle to find ambiguous solutions that would follow and yet subtly undermine the censor's demands.

THE CENSOR'S REPORT

The setting for the events and situations presented in the new novel by the writer Norman Manea is modern-day Bucharest, the year is 1980 according to specific statements ("three years after the earthquake"), but details suggest the immediate present. We are in a spring that follows a very severe winter, a time of extreme aggravation in people's moods and conditions, and at the same time a vigorous and lively spring in which the longing for life and love is felt with maximum intensity. People are seen in the ordinary activities of daily life, waiting at newsstands, walking in streets and parks, rushed and anxious, on trolleys and buses, talking about their needs and problems and in various situations at work.

The fortunes of several primary characters emerge through a number of scenes and a great deal of philosophical, historical, moral, and cultural commentary; the essential biographical data follows. New events occur in this spring that clarify the characters' past and present. *Anatol Dominic Vancea Voinov* appears with the greatest frequency: he is a former professor, presently employed as receptionist at the modest Hotel Transit, tolerated by his collective and his superiors for his knowledge for foreign languages. Intelligent, receptive, cultivated, Dominic, who in adolescence was a polite, timid, serious student, has become by this stage in his life shiftless, scatterbrained, indifferent to all that happens around him; he despises and makes fun of everyone; his language is violent and his style of dress offensive; he makes pretentious speeches in order to humiliate his colleagues, who are uneducated, simple people.

At heart Dominic, who has reached the age of fifty, is lonely, sad, and tired. Dissatisfied and disillusioned, he tries to resist a life of conformity and compromise through pretended indifference and mockery. His fate was determined by several misfortunes his family suffered in 1940: a lawsuit wrongly brought against them, followed by the disappearance of his father (murder or suicide?) after he received a threatening letter in the style of a Legion manifesto.[6] The family then broke up (the sister emigrated to Israel, the brother to Argentina, the mother died in poverty).

The search in which Dominic now engages, in this revitalizing spring, clarifies the family drama: the threatening letter that came in the black envelope was from a young man who in wartime had been in love with his sister and who later hid for almost forty years in an institution for deaf-mutes. No matter where Dominic searches, he cannot understand the past nor his feelings of guilt and their deep-seated causes. The main point of this search is the author's warning that small incidents can have lasting consequences on people in a time of violence, fear, and terror.

Another central character is *Matei (Mauriciu) Gafton,* a retired journalist. A believer during the period of dogmatism,[7] Gafton now tries to atone for the "lies" he wrote by sending anonymous petitions and letters calling irregularities, insufficiencies, and inaccuracies to the attention of the authorities in an attempt—as a "volunteer editor" placed in "the heart of events," "in touch with everything the man on the street is saying and thinking"—to reveal "the truth" and bring about "justice." At the same time, at the library he studies newspapers of the Fascist period, the Antonescu dictatorship,[8] with the intention of writing a monograph on "prewar

---

[6] Again, "Legion" refers to Romanian Fascist organizations like the Legion of the Archangel Michael.

[7] Party propaganda uses this term to refer to the Stalinist period.

[8] Originally aligned with the Legion, Gen. Ion Antonescu suppressed the Iron Guard when it tried to seize power. Antonescu's right-wing military dictatorship lasted until 1944, when Romania signed the armistice and changed sides to join the Allies.

and wartime disgust, and postwar enthusiasm and exaggeration" (p. 31). This character represents another version of living a lie: he changed his name during the war because he was Jewish, taking instead the name of his wife, who had a brother in the Fascist Legion who, after the war, became a wanted man. Gafton, "the endlessly persecuted, rejects the persecution of others" (pp. 218, 52, 56).

The antagonist of these two characters is *Ianuli*, the typical, consistent revolutionary, a complete character, an exemplary life. Originally from Greece, from a wealthy family, Ianuli broke with his people and with a university career and fought in the Greek mountains, gun in hand.[9] After the war he comes to Romania and throughout the passing years he holds to his youthful convictions, his pure "faith." Lacking any connection to his generation, unable to adapt to the new situation in Greece, living far from home and family, and not wishing to return since everything is changed there, Ianuli feels increasingly alienated, "marginalized." Now ill and resigned, betrayed by his wife, abandoned by all, he suffers acutely from the syndrome of isolation.

Two more characters are of primary importance for the understanding of the meaning of the novel.

One is *Dr. Marga*, a psychiatrist, a practical soul, a rationalist, confessor and adviser to those around him, a catalyst as they attempt to clarify their worries and doubts.

The other is *Irina Radovici*, through whom the problems of love are approached. Irina, an architect, capable and sensitive, has been pushed by events in her life onto the margins of society. Her coursework at the university was repeatedly interrupted, she was not permitted to take her final exams, she has been through two failed marriages; now she is working for the deaf-mute association's newspaper and trying to find the strength to escape from a love affair with no prospects by which she feels tyrannized. Her search for the balance that she seems to attain at the end of the book requires a continual estrangement from herself and from those around her, an exasperated opposition that takes all her energy; a restless and oppressive withdrawal from society; an austerity dominated by doubts and worries.

---

[9] Refers to the Greek civil war in the years immediately following World War II.

All these characters are in fact index cards for the projected novel by a strange writer, *Mynheer,* who is just now at an impasse. He wants to be inspired, to work, but he is isolated and apathetic; he is obsessed with writing the uncompromised truth about life and people, but at the same time he is filled with helplessness, doubt, and fear. The characters in the book are Mynheer's "substitutes," various attitudes, states of mind, and modes of existence that the author meets in his own life. Much space in the novel is devoted to Mynheer's wanderings through the streets of Bucharest, his conversations with various people, especially with *Toma* (an ambiguous character, an administrator and investigator), and his reflection on social, moral, cultural, and artistic subjects. The purpose of these interjections is to make explicit many of the ideas and theses presented in the novel: the need to make a clear choice (to choose between "Yes" and "No"); to live sincerely and authentically, and to condemn inauthenticity in society, in love, and in art; the relationships between truth and beauty, between the contemplative and the rational, between ideal and action, and so on.

A structural revision of the book will be necessary prior to publication, in order to clarify the ideological significance of certain themes and problems, and to permit the fuller development of main characters, their ability to become integrated into society, and the climate and external determinants of their existence.

A few suggestions:

1) The idea of the danger of the resurgence of the evil forces from the Fascist period under present-day conditions is present throughout the novel.

   For that very reason it must be treated with the greatest clarity.

   In the novel's present form this warning can be understood to refer to the situation in our country. Matei Gafton studies the Fascist Legion period and the Antonescu dictatorship in order to rouse the memories of those "who forget easily." He is worried and scandalized by the danger of a return to the past, by a tendency toward "amnesty for or just blurring of evil," by the temptation "to launch or relaunch evil"; he perceives the "errors," "the regressive ideas" of those "hiding" or "deforming" the truth about their involvement during the Fascist period.

There are repeated references in the novel to the media's knowledge of the robbing and burning of a woman's apartment on the pretext that she was keeping animals there.[10] The gravity of this violence, carried out in broad daylight under the impassive gaze of the militia, is stressed (pp. 10, 15, 32, 33, 34, 38, 39, 41, 47, 59, 60, 111, 219, 331). Toward the end of the book we learn that the entire family of the victim—*Mrs. Venera*—had been incinerated in Hitler's crematoria. Reconstructing the climate of the years before and during the war, Matei Gafton takes from the newspapers of the time only those headlines that show the creation of the mechanism of oppression during Antonescu's dictatorship, seeking evidence for the idea that the climate might have been generally favorable to the establishment of fascism[11] (pp. 13, 14, 30-31, 39, 47).

The scene in which Dominic imagines meeting ghosts from the past, people murdered or disappeared, including his father, is repeated many times. This is a one-sided approach, since there was a powerful anti-Fascist movement[12] in our country, as well as a democratically minded intelligentsia, and some measures were taken by the state itself[13] to save human lives during the deportations to Hitler's camps. The discussion at the end of the book between Dr. Marga and Ianuli on the psychology of isolation, on the distinctions ordinary people make in connection with those of other nationalities when problems or shortages are discussed (pp. 428, 433, 444–56), narrows the significance of the book.

The themes and ideas in the book—its ideological mes-

---

[10] During Ceauşescu's last years, the authorities tried to enforce a decree that forbade keeping domestic animals in apartment housing.

[11] Party propaganda refuses to recognize the great favor that right-wing and Fascist movements found with the electorate before World War II.

[12] One of the enduring clichés of Romanian propaganda is to exaggerate the (actually feeble) anti-Fascist movement in Romania before and during the war.

[13] In order to win the sympathy of the West during the last decade, the Party actually tried to touch up the picture of the Romanian right, especially its supposed humanitarian attitude toward minorities.

sage—would find fuller expression and be enriched by a plea
for involvement, for integration into a stable, authentic society, and by the positive development of characters in that
direction.

2) The novel presents a one-sided, preponderantly negative view
of daily life and of the social and moral climate in which the
fortunes of the characters evolve. Some contributing features:

a) Along with the central characters, who are mostly loners
unable to adapt, there are some significant secondary characters and situations: the cynical and opportunistic techno-
crat, lacking moral principles or conscience, who has a
function in the social hierarchy (pp. 95–98); opposite him,
the brilliant engineer who after graduating at the top of his
class turns down positions in the central government,
remaining an anonymous engineer in a small provincial
business to avoid making "concessions." Then there are
two aimless teenagers, amoral and loathsome: the boy,
who uses extremely vulgar language, is an alcoholic, confined to a psychiatric ward (pp. 83–88), while the girl,
accosted in the subway by a drunk, accepts his advances
(pp. 108–9).

b) Moral characterizations, personal relationships, the atmosphere in the workplace—to the degree these appear in the
novel—are all entirely odious. The personnel of the Hotel
Transit is made up exclusively of uneducated, primitive
types, loafers, backbiters, rumormongers, informers, and
bribe takers ("paid cockroaches") who cover up their dealings by arranging rooms for all kinds of important people
for their amorous trysts (pp. 70–78, 231–52). Anytime
doctors, nurses, or hospitals are mentioned, there is always
some insinuation of special deals, bribes, immorality
("gouging that had for some time been a part of this
once-noble occupation"). Examples: pp. 86, 317, 327, 361,
373.

The conversation between two officials, overheard in
the park by Irina Radovici, reveals the mechanism by

which an assembly for a Party election is arranged in a factory, and a general immorality (pp. 92–94).

c) Following the daily wanderings of the characters throughout the city and also through separate scenes, the novel presents an image of present-day Bucharest largely in negative, depressing, grotesque aspects: dirty, smelly streets, tired, aggressive people, primitivism, crowded trolleys and buses, lines outside grocery stores, mud, darkness, and the like.

The structure of the novel would permit a reexamination of all these elements and of the context that influences and determines the characters' states of mind. The image of Bucharest on beautiful spring days could provide a number of scenes and characters with a bright, invigorating background. Without such scenes the novel is flawed: it is one-sided. Modifying the text by the elimination of certain chapters, of some commentary, and excesses in the area of caricature, irony, and grotesquery, while rounding it out with the insertion of some positive, affirmative passages, would contribute to the balance and expression of the vision of the book as a whole.

Necessary clarifications of the significance of characters and the book's message.

• Dominic: He must understand at the end that indifference and living a lie are no solution: he should formulate at least a slight possibility of integration into society (he is after all the main character).

• Ianuli: This is a very important character (although he does not appear very frequently) for his ideological significance to the argument (the problems of foreigners, of the psychology of isolation, as well as the fate of professional revolutionaries who fight to defend their ideology). It should be made clear that his position as a revolutionary pushed out onto the fringes of society is due to the fact that he did not grasp the new problems and needs of our socialist period. This should be very explictly clarified. The conversations at the end and the narration throughout the novel, with regard to Ianuli's situation, should be reviewed, since in its present form his story could be understood to imply the failure of the socialist struggle in its latest stage, to imply the existence of an irreducible opposition between the revolutionary ideal and reality (see especially p. 424).

- Mynheer: He should have more the role of a "raisonneur" who helps to clarify the significance of the theoretical debates and the philosophical-sociological-moral reflections in the novel: he should argue for the importance of returning to the natural course of life, to a well-rooted stability, and for adopting a constructive way of behaving.

    The theme of "substitutes," which recurs on countless occasions—not only those concerning the relationship between the characters and the writer or the relationship between the characters and their real-life models—should be made clearer. In some formulations the notion of living a lie is wrongly extended to the whole of society. For example: "A substitute in a world of substitutes. . . . Each one found within himself the concept of substitution, *to be someone else, to escape from the self*" (p. 181). "Most of us become something else. If not the opposite of what we really are" (p. 184). "What substitutes are squeezed into still more substitutes?" (p. 322). "Substitute functions and substitute truth" (pp. 305, 306, 310, etc.).

The idea of the resurgence under present conditions of "the forces of evil," of the recurrence of certain phenomena pertaining to fascism, chauvinism, etc. The "warning."

- The problem should not be seen to reflect on our country. If included, it should be seen to reflect on the modern world (the media often show scenes of violent demonstrations in the West, neofascism, neonazism, etc. . . . and peace marches too, which could be seen and commented on by the characters).

- Literature, books, should not concern themselves with a

resurgence of nationalism and fascism. (For example, must Eminescu and Alecsandri[14] be brought to account? Must Rabbi Mozes R.?[15] There are the seeds of a great scandal here.)

- Gafton's research in the press (especially the year 1940) should not be limited to headlines about Romania, and should also include headlines marking the activities of the Romanian anti-Fascist movement and the protests of the democratically minded intelligentsia. King Carol and even Antonescu should not be placed on the same level as Hitler.[16]

- Care should be taken not to give the impression that there were murders, deportations, a real Holocaust in Romania (the image of rows of dead people repeatedly evoked by Dominic should be reviewed as well). It should not be forgotten that Romania was the only country that refused to deport Jews to the Nazi extermination camps.[17]

- Reduce the number of scenes and marginal comments on the news item taken from the Romanian press (was it?) concerning the devastation and *burning* of the woman's apartment, the animals being treated as a *pretext*. It should not be implied that the law enforcement agency—the Militia—would tolerate or "cover up" such an incident (we are not in West Germany).

- Review the last chapter of the book. The ending must be changed. Not emphasizing the syndrome of isolation and nationalist demonstration. This should not be the only problem explored in the book. In its present form the end

---

[14] Mihai Eminescu, Vasile Alecsandri: Romanian writers. There are some anti-Semitic lines in their works.

[15] Rabbi Mozes Rosen, a deputy in the Communist parliament for the last two decades, has in the last years protested the frequent publication of anti-Semitic texts by classic and contemporary Romanian authors.

[16] King Carol II initially agreed to collaborate with the Legion, then suppressed the movement. Forced to abdicate and leave Romania in 1940, the king turned over power to his heir King Michael (then nineteen) and General Antonescu.

[17] Party propaganda used this lie especially in order to win the sympathy of the West.

restricts and misdirects the readership. (In its present form, the book would be just for the initiate and of limited interest.) The theory of the psychology of isolation—as it is presented—can be summarized as follows:

- Foreigners in any society (normal or abnormal) retain distinctive characteristics that "should neither be denied nor used against them," that is, this is a "difference that must be accepted."

- The dominant or majority nationality do not consider foreigners to be equal. Under certain conditions ("unrest, crisis, worry, helplessness"), egotism, evil, and stupidity "explode and seek release" in selfish acts and attitudes (the same happens in situations of "generalized, institutionalized brutalization"???). Even under usual, everyday conditions certain phenomena indicate that normal interaction is relative: "you have equal rights to participate in evil, but not against evil"; it would be considered "an impertinence to try, as a foreigner, to teach those around you what is right"; the visitor "does not have the right to get too involved." . . . (Ianuli feels humiliated at the institute where he works because the people around him are surprised when "he himself" shows the courage to get involved in improving the organization.) In general, theorizing about the problem of nationalities should be avoided. We have laws and principles here. The problem of nationalities has been resolved in our country.

- Care should also be taken in the discussion of the question of going into exile as another form of "expatriation," undertaken out of a natural desire for "freedom," for change, from the horror of routine and "captivity." (The problem of "freedom" . . .) There are indirect reflections on this issue throughout the book.

Negative image of daily life.
The following chapters and scenes should be cut:
- pp. 63–67 (the chapter with the airplane and the description of the Chief of State—has no relevance to the problems explored in the book).

- pp. 83–84 (shorten the chapter dealing with the teenage alcoholic in the psychiatric ward).
- pp. 197–98 (the reference to the law reducing schooling for the handicapped "for reasons of economy").
- pp. 200–202 (excerpts from the deaf-mute newspaper; references to the principles on which the association of deaf-mutes is organized, that is on the basis of "democratic centralism," their statutes, etc.).
- pp. 214–15 (insults and blanket generalizations made in our country about Arab students).
- pp. 206–8 (the world as Dominic sees it).
- pp. 70–80, 231–52 (scenes at the Hotel Transit including the "arrangements" for important people). Also texts with generalizations about doctors. Some secondary characters (and why not a central one?) presenting a positive image must be added. At present there is only one scene of this type: a group of kindergarten children. And even they are presented as sad, lockstep automatons (p. 91).

The text must be modified in the following places:
- pp. 20, 24, 27, 44, 54, 61, 90, 91, 95, 96, 97, 98–100, 107, 114, 138–39, 217, 235, 263, 264, 266, 316, 326, 343, 346, 348 (images of streets, dirt, garbage, darkness, lines, shortage of merchandise, tired, brutalized people, chaos).
- pp. 12, 31, 89, 101, 268, 340 (repeated references to crowding in the transit system, p. 265: "the passenger struggles or accepts. To struggle is to accept, our local historians teach us").
- pp. 14, 77, 154, 194, 234, 245, 247, 302 (comments on the human condition, like this from pp. 311–12: "the working class has nothing to lose but its misfortunes").
- pp. 8, 10, 57, 200–201 (caricature of political language).
- p. 15 (theft of packages of foreign provenance at the post office), p. 29 ("the tyrants of this century," referring to Hitler and Stalin without distinguishing between them), pp. 54–55, 263 (Securitate), pp. 112, 353 (the law regarding dogs), p. 196 ("the Year of the Handicapped"), p. 222 ("sick of history"), pp. 353–55 (jokes, gossip).

Why was I afraid as I read? Was it the shock of coming face to face for the first time with a kind of "reading" I had only imagined, without ever having come across it? Did it stir an unconscious memory of a deeper fear, from the times of Nazi concentration camps and of Stalinist terror? Or were old memories stirred by the rumors circulating in Bucharest at the time, about the strange death of some of my fellow writers, about intellectuals and artists whose houses had been searched, and—especially—about an engineer whose diary was discovered and who was murdered while being interrogated by the Securitate?

My state of extreme overexcitement made me careless. That afternoon I had called my publisher at home to express my aston-ishment and indignation. "Is this it? This thing is supposed to save the book? Is this the kind of 'help' your miraculous person prom-ised us? The writing is supposed to be literary and professional—it reads like the 'new-style' sophomoric jargon of the 'new-style' police!"

There was a long silence. I realized I had acted imprudently. The phone of a "suspicious character" like me was sure to be tapped, and so was that of an "official" person like the director. "This reader's report has some suggestions. No one is forcing you to accept them. I don't see what you're so upset about." The words were spoken calmly, but he sounded embarrassed and nervous. "Come see me at the office tomorrow and let me know what you've decided," he said severely.

The next morning we met at his office together with the book's editor. The director's tone was official, as it had to be (all three of us assumed that there were Securitate listening devices somewhere in the room), but again I could not control my nerves.

At the end of the conversation the director did allow himself a moment of openness. "You know, every day, on every book we want to publish, we receive notes and reports and even complaints, sometimes much worse than the one you're so worried about. What would happen if we got scared every time? We'd never publish a single book. . . ."

Yes, we were all caught in the same squeeze: without the interaction of determination and duplicity, of personal relations and persistence, nothing at all could be done, not one of the books would have managed to slip through the fine net of the word police and be published.

Along with the editor, I started again the struggle of seeming to meet the censor's objections, at heart without meeting them.

The book was again forwarded to the censor's office in April 1986. It was my understanding that this time it would be read by a different reviewer. The new notes penciled on my typescript were followed by the direct request (relayed orally by the publisher, of course) that I drop other details of the deaf-mute association, and that I modify the "structure" of the character Ianuli (the former revolutionary behaved as a deaf-mute, not saying a word in the whole novel) and of the ending (which suggested that both this character and the main female character were at the point of suicide). This was the third set of changes I was asked to make. In the end the last censor sent a message that publication would be recommended. The censor had to appear at a special half-hour interview with the deputy minister of culture, where he would receive the final approval. This was the ritual with "problem" books.

The book came out in the summer of 1986. The publisher, strangled by the pressure from the censor's office, had to make a profit on every book it put out. Thus he printed twenty-six thousand copies. In twenty years as a published writer, I had never aspired to such an unusually large run. Most probably public interest was aroused by the rumors that flew around any time a book was held up and chopped up by the censor's office. The novel sold out in Bucharest in a few days. My friends assured me that even in the "substitute" version it had retained its critical acuity and literary originality. The first reviews, highly favorable, appeared in the country's main literary journals in the fall of 1986. In December 1986 I left Romania.

The substitute report helped me get my book published. And the

censor helped. Close friends and unknown enemies helped. Even
the dictator helped in his way, by promoting ambiguity and chaos,
a remove from the old-line political purity.

I am a writer who could not have been published during the
Stalinist era. My generation grew up in the ambiguous, tortured,
agonizing period (the "enlightened years") of the new dictatorship.
Our books struggled into being in the clear darkness, in a situation
that was constantly changing and increasingly threatening and suffocating.

Was I happy when I saw my newly published book? It had been
a difficult and unhoped-for birth. My crippled baby, though it was
not as I had imagined it, was still mine. The bonds that joined us,
strong and scarred, were of this time and place in which we struggled, mutilated ourselves, to stay on the surface.

The substitute censor's report probably requires no comment.
In considering the multilayered, duplicitous situation of Romania's recent and past history ("the eternity of the locus"), I
should perhaps begin by describing one of my few contacts with
the Securitate. An elegant young man from the "Writers Section"
offered me Kent cigarettes (which in Romania are seldom
smoked; they are used as a kind of currency on the black market);
he was polite and cool, he spoke openly. For more than an hour
he discussed . . . Faulkner. And discussed him competently, I must
admit. This confirmed the success that the Securitate had had in
recent decades in recruiting some of the best university graduates.
He soon told me that he had read all my books and "understood"
them, an emphasis that of course gave me no pleasure. ("Did you
think, for instance, that I didn't catch the references to Piero di
Cosimo and to the 'carnival' in the book you wrote ten years
ago?") I felt awkward, I fidgeted and searched for words, I felt
confused, alienated, like a stammering deaf-mute no longer sure
what world I lived in and why, in sharp contrast to him, so
relaxed, rational, and courteous, so receptive and well-intentioned.
Only at the end of this uncomfortable interview did he ask in
passing what I thought of various debates in the literary journals,

my views on certain "groups" and "lines of thought" and so on. No, he did not push it, this was no interrogation, nor did he force me to confess: it was just duplicitous conversation. He gave me an ironic, superior smile when I refused his invitation for another "friendly" get-together. . . .

To write a real commentary on the report I would have to comment on the long period, almost a quarter-century, of confusion and cryptic writing. That would be a whole book. But even a hasty comment should not leave out nor ignore the substitute report's "precious directions," some acknowledgement of its gracious faith in the irresistibility of correcting error, in a "moral" sense of order and proportion that would gradually lead the wanderer back to the right path. That strange creature—imprudent, excessive, sometimes incoherent—could still be co-opted, the shrewd censor-teacher reaffirmed patiently and optimistically. This was always the goal of education, to give advice, make reproaches, threats, observe faults, offer rewards. This is the education that is with us from birth—in the home, in school, in the army, in church, throughout marriage, in the Party—until death, and perhaps afterward. The "sensible advice" of the Authority fulfills the need for security and order felt by many of the citizens of every state, in whose upbringing the state has invested so much effort and hope.

> It is not the function of art to wallow in dirt for dirt's sake, never its task to paint men only in states of decay, to draw cretins as the symbol of motherhood, to picture hunchbacked idiots as representatives of manly strength. . . . Art must be the handmaiden of sublimity and beauty and thus promote whatever is natural and healthy. If art does not do this, then any money spent on it is squandered.

These words of common sense are not those of my censor (although they are very likely the opinions of all censors everywhere, including mine). Nor is this a quote from Senator Jesse Helms, with his concern lest obscenity and blasphemy somehow profit from state support of the arts. Nor are they words of the late

Ayatollah Khomeini, who condemned the novelist Salman Rushdie to death. Nor are they the commonsense reaction of Americans scandalized by the use of an American flag for a carpet at the entrance to an exhibit, and the growing numbers who favor repealing the right to insult the flag guaranteed by the U.S. Constitution. (Of course people of all nationalities are instructed from an early age to revere their country's flag and perhaps to burn or defile those of their enemies.) The above words could have been said by many, present or past; they were in fact spoken by Adolf Hitler in his fateful speech at Nuremberg in September 1935.

After I found the quote from Hitler I kept repeating it obsessively, for very personal reasons. I had been since the Nazi years of my childhood a "banned" person. Then came the nightmare of Stalinism, and the complicated failures of the always uncertain "thaws" that followed, and my confused and frustrated desires for freedom deepened. I might ask today, to what degree am I still qualified for liberty and its privileges?

The report accompanied me on my painful journey during the years after I left Romania. I reread the original manuscript of the novel, comparing it with the published substitute form. Co-opted by the system? No. Truncated or not, altered or not, "they" could not co-opt the text: it seemed I had won there.

But truncated and changed as it was, has the novel survived? Neither the favorable reviews that had begun to appear in Romania when I left, nor even an admiring comment in *Le Monde* that *The Black Envelope* continued in the Kafka tradition, could counteract the irritation I felt as I reread the book. It was not the disappearance from the edited version of various dark details of daily life that upset me, nor the "softening" of so many passages. It was the warping effect of all that encoding, obfuscation, stylistic excess and opacity, devitalization, circuitousness, and waste. The censor's office won as if by delayed action and remote control, even when I thought I had fooled and beaten them. The writer who thought himself so aesthetically "engaged" discovered any number of pages, fragments, chapters that had been corrupted by the very artifices he had used (often with a sense of triumph) as a defense against the censor's office. And he asked himself whether this was just the usual dissatisfaction of any author faced with a long-unfinished work, or whether it was more than that. . . .

A writer friend wrote me from Bucharest, on January 21, 1990: "What will last, of all the literature we have written, that was written in the last forty years? Is it only a contextual literature, of circumstantial value, when it exploits historical facts and even when it ignores them? I am a pessimist as you know: it could be that it will all form a 'parenthesis' in history, meaningless in the future and unintelligible to anyone who didn't live it."

This painful question mirrored another question I came across around the same time. This question was raised at the end of an article about postwar Romanian literature written by another friend, a Romanian literary critic living in Paris: "It [Romanian literature] found the strength to survive dictatorship; will it find the strength not to languish when there are no constraints? Nobody can answer this, but the question must be put."[18]

There is a price to be paid for defying tyranny, even through literature. Sometimes those who have paid it pay again later, and not a negligible price, in trying to discover and adjust to life in a democratic society. Both situations imply a commitment to liberty that is fundamental to mankind no matter how baffling its contradictions may sometimes be.

"Freedom is a more complex and delicate thing than force," Mann wrote. Those who went into exile half a century after the great German writer confirm anew the truth of those words. Will it soon be confirmed once more by the recently liberated people of Eastern Europe?

Diversity of choices, the rigors of competition, vulnerability and risk, the harsh laws of the marketplace and the thrill of adventure, the excesses and inhibitions that come out of the productive, per-

[18] Mircea Iorgulescu, "The Resilience of Poetry," *Times Literary Supplement,* January 19–25, 1990, pp. 61–62.

haps exaggerated dynamism of democracy—these are just a few of the aspects of a free society.

We are learning the price of freedom after learning that of tyranny. And we reaffirm by our wounded destiny the value of freedom, even when freedom reminds us how fragile its delicate articulations can be, how complex and relative the solutions.

Perhaps especially then.

Bard College
Spring 1990
Translated by Alexandra Bley-Vroman

FELIX CULPA

When he died in 1986 at the age of seventy-nine, Mircea Eliade was a famous scholar at the University of Chicago (the Sewell L. Avery Distinguished Service Professor in the Divinity School and professor in the Committee on Social Thought), an expert in the history of religion, and a well-known writer.

He was the author of some fifty books, including collections of short stories, novels, plays, essays, and countless articles. In addition he also published volumes on philosophy and religion. The four-volume *A History of Religious Ideas* probably remains his most famous work.

His passion for knowledge, for reading and writing, dates from his early high school years in Bucharest. He published his first article ("How I Found the Philosopher's Stone") in 1921, at the age of fourteen. After receiving his master's degree in philosophy from the University of Bucharest in 1928, he spent three years studying Indian culture and philosophy at the University of Calcutta. He considered India his greatest spiritual experience. "In India I discovered what I later came to refer to as cosmic religious feeling," he would write much later in *Ordeal by Labyrinth* (1978).

Eliade earned his Ph.D. at the University of Bucharest in 1933, with a thesis on Yoga. He was appointed assistant to Nae Ionescu, the university's famous professor of logic and metaphysics, and began his teaching career with a course called "The Problem of Evil in Indian Philosophy." Eliade was fascinated by his mentor and friend, even when Ionescu became a propagandist for Italian fascism and German national socialism and a passionate supporter of the Iron Guard, the extreme-right-wing Romanian nationalist movement.[1]

Following the suppression of the Iron Guard, Eliade—already an important figure in Romanian contemporary culture and himself a supporter of the Iron Guard—ran into trouble with the authorities. Nevertheless, in 1940 he was appointed cultural attaché to the Romanian legation in London. A year later, when Romania entered the war as a German ally, Eliade had to leave London and was sent to the Romanian legation in Lisbon.

When the war ended he remained abroad. He went to Paris, where he taught at the École des Hautes Études, and later lectured at various European universities before settling, in 1956, at the University of Chicago.

---

[1] Perhaps the best way to describe Nae Ionescu would be to combine the characterizations by Mac Linscott Ricketts, an American scholar of the Ionescu period, and Virgil Nemoianu, a Romanian literary critic who is currently a professor at the Catholic University in Washington, D.C.

"Nae Ionescu was by no means a simple propagandist of Italian Fascism or German National Socialism. His teachings and his activities do, however, situate him well within the ambit of the nationalistic, antidemocratic philosophies and movements of interbellum Europe generally known as fascist" (Mac Linscott Ricketts, *Mircea Eliade, The Romanian Roots, 1907–1945*, vol. 1 [Boulder: East European Quarterly, 1988], p. 114).

"A minor, but lively Socratic thinker, Ionescu advocated a kind of vitalistic existentialism (an irrationalism that was not foreign to concepts borrowed from Orthodox Christianity), preached the superiority of oral charisma over written philosophical communication, engaged in political journalism, and ended up as a supporter of the Iron Guard, the Romanian ultra-nationalist and extreme-right movement" (Virgil Nemoianu, "Mihai Şora and the Traditions of Romanian Philosophy," *Review of Metaphysics* [The Catholic University of America], vol. 42 [March 1990], p. 596).

Among the many crimes arranged by the Legion, or Iron Guard, must be mentioned the barbarous ritual murder of two hundred Jews, including children, on January 22, 1941, at the Bucharest slaughterhouse (while the "mystical" murderers sang Christian hymns), an act of ferocity perhaps unique in the history of the Holocaust. Ion Antonescu, their former ally, later dissolved the Iron Guard, but anti-Semitic murders did not cease under his military dictatorship. There were, to name but two, the terrible pogrom in Iaşi in June 1941, when thousands of Jews were murdered and thousands more put on the "death trains" to die of asphyxiation, and the deportation in 1941 and 1942 of the Jews of Bukovina and Bessarabia in northeastern Romania to the "Transnistria" extermination camps in the western Ukraine, then occupied by Romanian troops allied with Hitler's Germany.

His journals and his autobiography, published in the 1980s, offer interesting insights into his life and work. Unfortunately, they do not *demystify* the ideological and political stands he took during the Fascist period. In another context, Eliade maintained that "a demystifying attitude is altogether too facile." He was more interested in "the camouflage adopted by the sacred in a desacralized world," as he wrote in *Ordeal by Labyrinth.* "I made the decision long ago to maintain a kind of discreet silence as to what I personally believe or don't believe."

In 1937, however, Eliade had written in the journal *Vremea* that "To me, then, it is a matter of complete indifference whether Mussolini is or is not a tyrant. Only one thing interests me: that this man has transformed Italy in fifteen years, turning a third-rate state into one of the world powers of today." At the time he was a staunch admirer of Mussolini and Corneliu Codreanu,[2] the "captain" of the Iron Guard. Obsessed since his youth with the relationship between the sacred and the profane, Eliade could hardly have predicted the terrible consequences of his views. It is difficult to know whether and in which direction his views evolved in the postwar years. However, we do know through his writings that his skepticism toward the Western model of democracy remained constant throughout his life.

His brilliant scholarly work broadened the understanding of myths, archetypes, and of the history of religion (all favorite subjects of his). It is not surprising therefore that despite his persistent anticommunism, Eliade the scholar was able to agree, in an interview, that Mao could be seen as "the last emperor," "the guardian and interpreter of the right doctrine and, in everyday life, the person responsible for his people's peace and well-being," that "the myth

---

[2] Corneliu Zelea-Codreanu (1899–1938). Anti-Semite and far-rightist agitator, founder and leader of the Iron Guard. Imprisoned under King Carol II in 1938, Codreanu was garroted and shot "while attempting to escape."

of Stalin reveals a nostalgia for the archetype," or that Lenin's tomb, not at all religious in essence, "does perform the function of a religious symbol." He added to these comments, which appeared in *Ordeal by Labyrinth,* that "there is no 'degradation' that does not reflect a lost, or confusedly desired, higher state."

It is not by chance that Eliade, otherwise a relatively humorless man, liked Federico Fellini's *The Clowns;* he praised it "for re-creating the great mythic themes and making use of certain major symbols in unusual forms." Eliade searched for sacredness, for magic, for mystery, even when it led to mystification.

It would have been a welcome surprise if in his later autobiographical writings he had contradicted his earlier position and made an attempt to "demystify" his involvement with totalitarian ideology. The final volume of the journals,[3] published in 1990, was his last chance, but he did not take it. Of course, there is always the possibility that such a surprise may be found among his as yet unpublished writings. But in the context of the recent political changes in Eastern Europe—changes stimulated and led by some admirable writers and artists, who fought courageously against tyranny—it is tragic that these words do not seem to exist.

As we know, the number of intellectuals on the "wrong" side—the side of totalitarianism—was not at all negligible in the last half-century. Even now, during Eastern Europe's transition to a civil society, there are voices that speak for the necessity of "good doctrine" and "iron discipline," the necessity for a powerful state, for a sacred authority, etc. Once more, the ghost of the tyrant buffoon is looking for his crowd of supporters and is haunting his old servants, the profane clowns ready to acclaim his absurd sanctity.

The fight against the canonizing of power seems to be as difficult as ever. Certainly, had Eliade testified to his involvement, as a

---

[3] Mircea Eliade, *Journal IV: 1979–1985,* trans. Mac Linscott Ricketts (Chicago: The University of Chicago Press, 1990).

thinker and believer, with the totalitarian ideology and movement, his thoughts on the experience could have had a great impact, especially at this moment.

Eliade's fourth and last volume of his journals fits smoothly into the pattern of the previous books. It is of modest length and ends shortly before his death. Again we find the same structure: the important and less important events of the day are noted laconically and tied to his scholarly and literary work, to his teaching, his travels, conferences, people he comes in contact with, and so on. The observation made by Larry McMurtry[4] in connection with an earlier volume applies here as well: "This is not a journal of personality, much less of gossip. Eliade doesn't give the impression that he is too good, either for personality or for gossip, but merely that he is too busy, too absorbed by the work at hand."

The journal even includes a datebook, which it sometimes resembles, as the author himself acknowledges; yet it also reveals some private moments of melancholy and even of suffering. With advancing age, Eliade sometimes abandons his discretion, strategies, and impersonal attitude. In the entry for November 19, 1983, we find the following disturbing admission: "I can't lift heavy books from the shelves, I can't rummage the file folders. . . . Why have I been punished for—and through—those things I have loved all my life: books and writing?"[5] In general he connected his melancholy to lack of energy. "I suffer from melancholy provoked, as usual, by . . . what I *must* do now, immediately" (March 31, 1979).[6]

The reader of *Journal IV* is often aware of the burdens of age and illness, the diminution of the extraordinary capacity for very diverse work that Eliade retained throughout his long life. The presenti-

[4] Larry McMurtry, quoted in Mircea Eliade, *Journal II: 1957–1969* (Chicago: The University of Chicago Press, 1989).

[5] Eliade, *Journal IV*, p. 75.

[6] Eliade, *Journal IV*, p. 10.

ment of the end is tempered by discretion and retrospection, often from lofty heights.

If we had to pick out the underlying motifs running through the feverish activity described in the journals, we would probably settle on two major obsessions that characterized Eliade's last years, as they did indeed his whole life: books and Romania. As Wendy Doniger correctly emphasizes in her affectionate epilogue to volume four, for Eliade "the primary focus is books; people come second."[7] The drama of the approaching end focuses on the books that he will not be able to write more than on the people from whom he must part. There are passages in *Journal IV* that touch painfully on the inevitability of the end; others, in striking contrast, show Eliade's very restrained, cool side, for instance the description of the calm and meticulous care with which he divided up his library. Together these two sides compose a memorable portrait of the scholar. It seems likely that the people closest to him must have found it difficult to compete with the books he lived with so intimately; books were the ruling passion of his life, from an adolescence of insatiable reading (he developed a system by which he gradually cut sleep to a minimum in order to make more time for reading and writing) through his insomniac old age, when the magic of books still had the power to revitalize him.

The vast body of knowledge he acquired through reading made Eliade an erudite and encyclopedic figure, the ideal person to entrust with editing *The Encyclopedia of Religion.* His rate of intellectual production was extraordinary.

Since he saw books as magically connected to life, there was an odd relationship between the destruction of his books and his coming death. A dream he describes on July 21, 1979, included these typically surrealist elements: an elegant gentleman in a copy shop, surrounded by a multitude of bizarre little animals, a manuscript

---

[7] Wendy Doniger, epilogue to Eliade, *Journal IV,* p. 149.

being reduced to a sandwich for mice who cannot be stopped from eating it, the author's panic, and so on. This nightmare actually came true, or at least had an echo in the mysterious fire that destroyed Eliade's office library at Chicago's Meadville-Lombard School of Religion on December 19, 1985, four months before his death. Dream and reality are thus joined in a somber warning that time is running out. Eliade describes the harsh ringing of the telephone, the panic, the fire fighters, the water flooding the stairs to his office. The old man paralyzed in the chill night air, in the face of disaster, the figure diminished by age and illness, sets a scene of tragic finality.

It seems probable, as Doniger suggests,[8] that Eliade considered his work more important than his life. Nevertheless, that he considered his life meaningful, as indeed it was, is clear from the fact that he published so many memoirs and journals recording its events— he was not, as might be thought, a scholar who built an impenetrable wall of books between himself and the real world.

To the end of his life, Eliade wrote his literary works and memoirs in Romanian. His relationship with the Romanian language and culture, as well as with Romanians living at home and abroad (it is remarkable how many he kept in touch with, even at this advanced age, from like-minded thinkers to Communist officials to admirers and students of his work to friends and relations, even absolute strangers), reflects a lively and lasting interest—and more than that, a deep sense of affiliation. That Eliade spent more than half his life outside of Romania and writing in other languages only underscores this fact.

This sense of affiliation can also be seen in the relationship he maintained with Romania and *Romanianism*[9] in this volume as in

---

[8] Doniger, epilogue to Eliade, *Journal IV*, p. 153.

[9] "Romanianism," however, was a term that in the mind of the public was associated with ultra-right-wing political philosophies and programs. All the parties of the extreme right—the Cuza Nationalist, the Legion, etc.—invoked it in their propaganda. Ordinarily it signified chauvinism, anti-Semitism, policies for the restraint of minorities, anticommunism, and enthusiasm for Italian fascism and German national socialism. Eliade believed

the preceding ones, a fact that should be stressed for other reasons
too: he represents *a case,* a case with broad significance for
Romanian intellectual life and even for the fate of Romania in the
future.

During his life, perhaps especially toward the end, Eliade constantly thought about his relationship with the country he had left
but could never leave behind. "I kept thinking of what I would have
suffered had I remained in the homeland as professor and writer,"
Eliade noted, with odd candor, on October 10, 1984, "if it hadn't
been for that *felix culpa:* my adoration for Nae Ionescu and all the
baleful consequences (in 1935–1940) of that relationship."[10] The
thought was repeated, virtually in the same formulation, in the last
pages of this journal: "I think of myself: without that *felix culpa*
(being a disciple of Nae Ionescu), I'd have remained in the homeland. At best, I'd have died of tuberculosis in a prison" (August 29,
1985).[11] Eliade, the great scholar of religion, refers most probably to
St. Augustine's line: *O felix culpa, quae talen ac tantum meruit
habere Redemptorem* (O happy guilt, which has served such a great
Redeemer.)

It is at best very naive to imagine that Eliade's adoration of the Iron
Guard ideologue Nae Ionescu would have been the only reason for
which he could have been arrested after the war by the Communists, although it would indeed have been sufficient cause. If an
excuse were needed (thousands were arrested without one), it could
easily have been found in Eliade's journalistic activity at the time
the Iron Guard was in ascension, when the left-wing press called

---

that the word, which he found in the writings of the nineteenth-century nationalists he
admired, notably Kogălniceanu, Eminescu, and Haşdeu, had originally signified something "above politics, and that it had been debased by political parties in the twentieth
century" (Ricketts, *Mircea Eliade, The Romanian Roots,* p. 904).

[10] Ricketts, *Mircea Eliade, The Romanian Roots,* p. 104.

[11] Ricketts, *Mircea Eliade, The Romanian Roots,* p. 142.

him a "Fascist" and a "Legionnaire."[12] A number of other serious
charges could have been brought against him: his attacks on communism and on the Soviet Union, his disputes with the left-wing
press, and his scandalous sanctification of the "martyrs" of the
Spanish civil war (those who fought for Franco, of course).[13] As
serious was his eulogy of Antonio de Oliveira Salazar, the dictator
of Portugal,[14] whom he saw as a "model" for the dictator Ion
Antonescu. That book on Salazar was written and published in 1942
while Eliade worked at the Romanian legation in Lisbon—a position that in itself could have been the basis for an indictment. His
file would have been filled to bursting had the Communist authorities wanted to justify severe punishment. Of the accusations of
fascism continually brought against Eliade by the left-wing press,
Ricketts writes, "In a sense, Eliade's critics—unjust though they
were—saw more clearly than he himself the direction in which his
thinking was taking him."[15] It is certainly hard to believe that any
miracle of the kind that had spared Eliade in 1940—when the
leaders of the Iron Guard movement, including Nae Ionescu, were
arrested—could have been repeated under the Communist regime.

---

[12] "The later prominent Communist poet M.R. Paraschivescu (1911–1971) interpreted
Huliganii [*The Hooligans,* Eliade's novel—N.M.] as having been written under the
influence of Heidegger, 'the official philosopher of Hitlerism.' He found in the novel an
all-pervading atmosphere of *death,* which he attributed to the Heideggerian influence"
(Ricketts, *Mircea Eliade, The Romanian Roots,* p. 1033).

Ricketts also cites I. Constantinovschi (p. 1034), Andrei Şerbulescu (B. Silber) (pp. 694,
894), again Paraschivescu (pp. 895–97), and Alexandru Sahia (pp. 694, 1334). The reader
should certainly also keep in mind the opinion of Lucreţiu Pătrăşcanu, *Sub trei dictaturi*
(*Under Three Dictatorships*) (Bucharest: Editura Politică, rev. ed. 1970, p. 54). As late as
1971, Miron Constantinescu, another longtime Communist leader, counted Eliade
among the "ideological standard-bearers" of the Iron Guard (in *Magazin istoric* [*History
Journal*] 1, Bucharest, January 1971, p. 75).

[13] Mircea Eliade, "Ion Moţa ţi Vasile Marin" ("Ion Moţa and Vasile Marin"), in *Vremea,*
Bucharest, January 24, 1937. Mircea Eliade, "Comentarii la un Juràmint" ("Comments
on an Oath"), in *Vremea,* Bucharest, February 21, 1937.

[14] Mircea Eliade, *Salazar si revoluţia în Portugalia* (*Salazar and the Revolution in Portugal*)
(Bucharest: Editura Gorjan, 1942).

[15] Ricketts, *Mircea Eliade, The Romanian Roots,* p. 897.

If his health had somehow withstood the hard years of imprison-
ment, Eliade would have been freed in the sixties, like others who
had shared his way of thinking. Like them he would then have
become the beneficiary of the new policy of "retrieved" values. He
could have been allowed to publish at least some portions of his old
and of his new books, he would have been favored with respect and
with "tolerance" reserved for some "useful" Romanian intellectuals, he might even have received the calculated "encouragement" of
officials, for whom the ideas of their former political opponents
now provided useful sources of justification for their own system.
The ideological apparatus of Ceauşescu's party began a systematic
study of the Iron Guard movement, envying its former popularity
and using its slogans as its own. "The national revolution," with all
its chauvinistic emphasis, replaced the idea of internationalism. The
totalitarian state was to center around a "Conducător" (Leader); it
started a discrediting campaign against democracy, against intellectuals, against criticism, it repressed liberalism, and so on.[16] The
enemy of Ceauşescu's Fascist-Communist party was not right-wing
extremism but democracy. The democratic and rationalist trends in
Romanian thought (that is, the principles of the democratic-bour-
geois revolution of 1848, the sarcastic humor of the great Romanian
writer Ion Luca Caragiale, the legacy of the literary critic and social
thinker Eugen Lovinescu, and so on)[17] began to be a favorite target

[16] "The experiment and popularization of the Iron Guard has become an object of study
and a source of inspiration upon which the Bovarism of the Communist Party can feed,
finally, without interdiction.

"The adoption and revival of the traditional nationalistic clichés that were used with
such great and proven popularity by the Iron Guard in the Thirties . . . the basic
principles of the Legion, the same as the basic principles of the Communist Party: eulogy
of the national revolution and of the totalitarian state, cult of blind obedience to the
beloved 'leader,' anathemization of the democratic system, discrediting the critical and
libertarian approach, and justification of the repression of intellectual liberalism" (Ileana
Vrancea, "Capcana" ["The Trap"], in *Dialog,* Dietzenbach, Federal Republic of Germany, September 1989, p. 19).

[17] "The militant anti-totalitarianism of Romanian intellectuals in the period between the
wars as they promoted freedom of thought and rejected any sabotage, is still today, as
in the past, the real enemy of and principal threat to the Communist dictatorship, while

of "witch-hunters," as were of course the "decadent influences" of the West, around which the omnipresent Securitate strove to throw a cordon sanitaire. We do not know whether Eliade would have reacted the same way as Constantin Noica, a brilliant philosopher and scholar whom neither years in Communist prisons nor his earlier right-wing affiliation brought to repudiate the Ceauşescu regime. With his Platonic mistrust of democracy and his fascination with "the Romanian soul" and with "pure" intellectual rigor, Noica criticized Western "decadence" more frequently and more sharply (it was after all more comfortable to do so) than he criticized Ceauşescu's dictatorship. Noica's death shortly after Eliade's was regarded as a great loss by the entire Romanian intellectual community, not only by his fervent admirers—who paradoxically included some of the most upright opponents of Ceauşescu's regime as well as many of its most abject supporters.

Eliade never returned to Romania, and his destiny must be viewed from that perspective. In the West, his status as an anti-Communist most probably protected him for a while from unpleasant questions or reproaches in connection with his relationship to fascism, but these did come later. However, they were not raised under the terrible punitive threat of the Communist enemy, but by the democratic society he had always regarded with deep skepticism. In any case they required a reply. Since his answers were evasive and unsatisfactory, the questions persisted. This pursuit was by no means pleasant, even if it was not as dramatic as it might have been under a totalitarian system.

Echoes of these annoying confrontations appear in this last volume of the journals. "I learned that Furio Jesi has devoted a chapter of calumnies and insults to me in his book that has come

---

the anti-democratism and anti-individualism of the extreme right, with its cults of sabotage and of mass obedience, is its greatest ally," (Vrancea, "Capcana" ["The Trap"], p. 23).

out recently, *Cultura di destra* [*Culture of the Right*]. I learned long ago that Jesi considers me an anti-Semite, fascist, Iron Guardist, etc. Probably he accuses me also of Buchenwald. . . . It makes no difference to me if he abuses me in his book (I shan't read it, and therefore I won't respond to it)" (June 6, 1979).[18] His irritation is so great that he drops his cool scholarly tone to label as calumnious a book that he has not read and does not intend to, and he invokes Buchenwald in a wry tone that is at best inappropriate. Even when he resumes his blasé mask, we find only a slippery reply: "Barbă-neagră relates to me that Jean Servier said to him recently: that from Israel they have received precise instructions that I am to be criticized and attacked as a fascist, etc. Jean Servier, says Barbăneagră, was indignant. . . . I believe it, but there's nothing to be done" (July 4, 1979).[19]

Is this annoyance—passed off as irony or transmuted into tired self-pity—a sign of vulnerability, of guilt, or of some higher detachment from petty questions?

To those who came to know Eliade, in his exile, as an affable émigré of delicate sensibilities and stylized civility ("the last man in the world to have a totalitarian thought," said a friend), such accusations were inconceivable. It is not easy to find a strategy to elude this kind of accusation if it cannot be proven false. In mankind's outraged memory, nazism is characterized not merely by its racist ideology or by its militancy, but especially by the catastrophic consequences of Hitler's hysterical propaganda—arrogant brutality, devastating warfare, extermination camps. But this infamous human tragedy has to be seen in the context in which it arose. In a period of acute economic, political, moral, and intellectual crisis, national socialism offered a simplistic, violent, and "radical" solution. Nazism, a very dark ideology from the beginning, did not at

[18] Eliade, *Journal IV,* p. 17.
[19] Eliade, *Journal IV,* p. 20.

first mean crematoria; it developed slowly, slyly, cruelly, to its sinister culmination. Seemingly at the opposite pole lies communism, which derives its militant demagogy and terror from the *humanism* of an egalitarian and rationalist utopia—a distinction that should never be overlooked, even in context of the Gulag.

As we strive to understand the collective or individual guilt for nazism, we have to look to those who understood the horror from the start. There were those who grasped the monstrous nature of the totalitarian plan before its outcome became generally known. At least one pre-Holocaust opinion should be cited, not that of a philosopher or of a writer but of a journalist who saw with clarity the relationship between national socialist ideology and the daily reality of Hitler's Germany. The American journalist Dorothy Thompson, who was expelled from Germany for her anti-Nazi writing, considered nazism "a repudiation of the whole past of Western man. . . . In its joyful destruction of all previous standards; in its wild affirmation of the 'Drive of the Will'; in its Oriental acceptance of death as the fecundator of life and of the will to death as the true heroism, it is darkly nihilistic. Placing will above reason; the idea over reality; appealing, unremittingly, to totem and taboo; elevating tribal fetishes; subjugating and destroying the common sense that grows out of human experience; of an oceanic boundlessness, Nazism . . . is the enemy of whatever is sunny, reasonable, pragmatic, common-sense, freedom-loving, life-affirming, form-seeking and conscious of tradition."

It would be tremendously enlightening to have Eliade respond to Dorothy Thompson's understanding of the Fascist philosophy and system, especially because Romanian fascism was a Christian Orthodox movement with specific links to Christian ethics, to the "Oriental" vision of a heroic death, to the "Drive of the Will," and to the tribal rituals of blind subjection to the chief. Who could better explain than Eliade why so many of the eminent intellectuals of his generation opted for this sinister involvement, and how a conservative intellectual is transformed into an extremist thinker? It would be as revealing as explaining the evolution of a humanistic, "progressive" intellectual into a simplistic and militant Communist. Does the explanation lie simply in the confusion of a society in crisis, a society that had not yet built a solid democratic foundation?

Eliade always avoids any clear analysis of his period of militancy; on this potentially unpleasant matter he prefers ambiguity and evasiveness. (Even in less controversial areas, as for example scholarly questions regarding the history of religions, he puts off or sidesteps direct confrontation and open debate.) When labeled "Nazi" or "anti-Semite," his reaction to the crushing weight of accusations that after all make a brutal simplification of his life story is to withdraw. There is an eloquence as well as a dignity in silence; there is delicacy in evasion, not just cunning; but we cannot avoid seeing that in silence and evasion there is much that is also reprehensible. What about publicly retracting one's former beliefs, denouncing the horrors, disclosing the mechanisms of mystification, assuming the guilt? Perhaps very few people are sufficiently lucid and courageous for this, and it is these few who deserve to be called people of conscience. To be truly separated from past errors one must acknowledge them. Is not *honesty,* in the final analysis, the mortal enemy of totalitarianism? And is not conscience (critical examination in the face of uncomfortable questions; in short, the results of a lucid, ethical engagement) conclusive proof of one's distance from the forces of corruption, from the totalitarian ideology? These forces are not necessarily either simple or direct, and often they act on human vulnerability in complex and indirect ways. In his recently published autobiography, Andrei Sakharov confessed his youthful admiration for Stalin. That admission has its origin in a fundamental honesty that has gradually enabled this great scientist and humanist to achieve a profound understanding of the nature of the Communist system and to become its unyielding critic—unyielding in spite of all he suffered; a shining symbol, an inspiration to all intellectuals of this tortured century.

But when questions do not arise from one's own conscience, they come from without. Is it surprising that only Eliade's "enemies" asked awkward questions? Would it be natural for his admirers, before anyone else, to have been his most exacting judges? Once more, on July 23, 1979, he refers to Furio Jesi. "C. Poghirc comes to see me. . . . He talks also about the campaign against me in Italy, provoked by Furio Jesi. The aim: to eliminate me from among the favorites for the Nobel Prize."[20]

Those who bear honest witness to the totalitarian tragedy come from among the victims and only rarely from among the guilty parties. If these "guilty" witnesses could reveal the essentials of the monstrous banality of evil, we could probably not only understand more thoroughly the past but also have a better idea of the future of humanity. But people prefer to talk about innocent suffering rather than their responsibility in the general suffering.

"Between a tradition of thought and the ideology that inscribes itself, always abusively, within it, there is an abyss," write Philippe Lacoue-Labarthe and Jean-Luc Nancy in their very interesting study, "The Nazi Myth."[21] We may have reason to question this categorical claim and in particular the advisability of the term "abyss," but the argument suggested by this provocative text should be followed attentively.

> Nazism is no more in Kant, in Fichte, in Hölderlin, or in Nietzsche (all of whom were thinkers solicited by Nazism)—it is, at the extreme, no more even in the musician Wagner—than the Gulag is in Hegel or in Marx. Or the Terror, with all simplicity, in Rousseau. In the same way, and whatever its mediocrity (by whose measure its ignominy must however be weighed), Pétainism is not a sufficient reason to invalidate, for example, Maurice Barrès and Paul Claudel. Only to be condemned is the thought that puts itself deliberately (or confusedly, emotionally) at the service of an ideology behind which it hides, or from whose strength it profits: Heidegger during the first

---

[20] Eliade, *Journal IV*, p. 22.
[21] Philippe Lacoue-Labarthe and Jean-Luc Nancy, "The Nazi Myth," in *Critical Inquiry* 16, no. 2 (Winter 1990), p. 293.

ten months of Nazism, Céline under the Occupation, and a good many others, at that time or since (and elsewhere).[22]

"A good many others . . . and elsewhere," indeed. Romanian fascism—different though it may be from Hitler's or Mussolini's—still has the same principal characteristic: "an amalgam between rebellious emotions and reactionary social ideas," as Wilhelm Reich put it.[23]

The extremes of nationalism and militancy that gave rise to the Iron Guard (and its earlier and later variations) could already be observed in the (then still happy) confusion following the Treaty of Versailles after World War I, when Greater Romania was created. The inclusion of the new provinces, Transylvania, Bukovina, and Bessarabia, suddenly added to the country not only a large number of Romanians who formed the majority in those provinces, but also significant minority populations (Hungarians, Jews, Germans, and others). So it was not frustration over defeat, as in the case of Germany, nor discouraged inertia, as in Italy, but success that turned an ancient Romanian nationalism into violent, fanatical, and unfortunately all the more successful extremism. Violently anti-Semitic Romanian fascism, calling itself "Christian" and "moral," took advantage of a fragile, demagogic parliamentary democracy and sought its electoral base among the peasants, who were neglected and frustrated at a time when Romania was embarking on industrialization and modernization. The movement was responding to the same appeals as Hitler's national socialism: *find an identity* (which in the context of that confused period was as understandable for the Romanians as for the Germans) and *construct a mythology* (in the case of Romania, Christian Orthodoxy as the ideal of purity, utopian brotherhood, and so on and so forth). These slogans also offered Romanians a mechanism of identifica-

---

[22] Lacoue-Labarthe and Nancy, "The Nazi Myth," p. 295.

[23] Wilhelm Reich, *The Mass Psychology of Fascism* (New York: Farrar, Straus & Giroux, 1970), p. xiv.

tion.[24] Today we would call it Christian Orthodox fundamentalism with a terrorist structure, for it ritualized a cult of death and of Christian sacrifice, violently excluded all "foreigners," idealized pastoral life, and rejected democracy, individuality, and modern Western civilization.

Many of these ideas could already be found in the traditions of conservative Romanian thought. Important Romanian writers have expressed such a vision in journalism and philosophy. Leading names in Romanian culture, from the national poet Mihai Eminescu through B. P. Haşdeu, Nicolae Iorga, Octavian Goga, and more recently Eliade and Noica, were claimed as standard-bearers for the right-wing extremist movements. Naturally, their political writings did not directly incite their readers to genocide, although their intolerant and hate-filled language reached unbearable levels of violence in some texts.

"Mac Ricketts has come for three days. . . . Two evenings we dined together. He keeps asking me questions. There are periods still only partially understood: for example, the accusation and allusions to my 'Nazism' (anti-Semitism) in the years 1938 and 1939. I try to explain for him certain articles, conversations, and events of those years," Eliade mentions in the entry for March 5–8, 1984.[25] A former student of Eliade's at the University of Chicago, Ricketts has devoted two massive volumes of extraordinarily thorough documentation to his mentor.

Even if he does not always grasp the implications of Romania's Byzantine political atmosphere and all the historical ramifications of nationalism in its Christian Orthodox variant, with the ongoing problems of mixed population and identity crisis, Ricketts provides a large quantity of carefully researched material and draws fair and balanced conclusions. He lists precisely the instances of violence by the Iron Guard or its oppressive fanatical strategies from which Eliade dissociated himself. In the end, Ricketts accepts the truth

---

[24] Lacoue-Labarthe and Nancy, "The Nazi Myth," p. 296.

[25] Eliade, *Journal IV,* p. 79.

revealed by the documents he so passionately studied. "Many of the
ideals of the Legion were identical to those Eliade had long been
advocating."[26] "Returning to one of his favorite themes, the mission
of Romania, he finds it embodied in the Legion's Program."[27] "In
his new-found enthusiasm for the Legion, which for years he had
classed as just another right-wing political extremist group, Eliade
lost his sense of perspective and overlooked the flaws in its doc-
trines and practices."[28] "Eliade wrote about the 'new aristocracy'
being constituted by the Legion."[29] "The longest pro-Legionary
article bearing Eliade's name is one that he has denied writing.
. . . Actually, the pseudonymous piece probably contains nothing
Eliade would not have agreed to at that time; it appears, in fact, to
have been based very closely on articles he had written in recent
years. . . . There can be no doubt at this time he did hope and believe
in the triumph of the Legionary movement."[30] Finally Ricketts
summarizes Eliade's view:

"Democracy has been unable to inspire in the people a spirit of
fervent nationalism—to make of them a strong, virile, optimistic
nation, imbued with a sense of mission and destiny. Being a foreign
import, democracy is concerned with matters that are not specifically Romanian concerns: with 'abstractions' such as individual
rights, rights of minorities, and freedom of political consciousness—and these, Eliade says, do not strike at the heart of 'Romania's problem.' "[31]

Ricketts also gives the Western reader significant quotations
from Eliade's journalism:

"We know of several tyrants who have transformed stupefied
countries into powerful states: Caesar, Augustus, and Musso-

[26] Ricketts, *Mircea Eliade, The Romanian Roots*, p. 920.
[27] Ricketts, *Mircea Eliade, The Romanian Roots*, p. 924.
[28] Ricketts, *Mircea Eliade, The Romanian Roots*, p. 925.
[29] Ricketts, *Mircea Eliade, The Romanian Roots*, p. 926.
[30] Ricketts, *Mircea Eliade, The Romanian Roots*, p. 929.
[31] Ricketts, *Mircea Eliade, The Romanian Roots*, p. 900.

lini."[32] "To me, then, it is a matter of complete indifference whether Mussolini is or is not a tyrant ... it is entirely immaterial what will happen to Romania after the liquidation of democracy. If, by leaving democracy behind, Romania becomes a strong state, armed, conscious of its power and destiny—history will take account of this deed."[33] "The Legion member is a new man, who has discovered his own will, his own destiny. Discipline and obedience have given him a new dignity, and unlimited confidence in himself, the Chief, and the greater destiny of the nation."[34] "There are a great many revolutionary impulses that have been waiting for thousands of years to be put into practice. That is why the Son of Man descended: to teach us permanent revolution."[35]

Other excerpts from pieces Eliade published in the Romanian press of the time could have been included too, such as the following:

In the name of this Romania that began many thousands of years ago and will not end until the apocalypse, social reforms will be enacted with considerable brutality, every corner of the provinces now overrun with foreigners will be recolonized, all traitors will be punished, the myth of our State will extend all across the country, and the news of our strength will stretch beyond its borders.[36]

Or this:

From those who have suffered so much and been humbled for centuries ... by the Hungarians—after the Bulgarians the most

---

[32] Eliade, "Democraţia şi problema Romaniei" ("Democracy and the Romanian Problem"), in *Vremea,* Bucharest, December 18, 1937.

[33] Eliade, "Democraţia şi problema României" ("Democracy and the Romanian Problem").

[34] Eliade, "Noua aristocraţie legionară" ("The New Legionary Aristocracy"), in *Vremea,* Bucharest, January 23, 1938.

[35] Eliade, "Cîteva cuvinte mari" ("A Few Big Words"), in *Vremea,* Bucharest, June 10, 1934.

[36] Eliade, "Democraţia şi problema României" ("Democracy and the Romanian Problem").

imbecilic people ever to have existed—from these political leaders of heroic martyred Transylvania, we await a nationalist Romania, frenzied and chauvinistic, armed and vigorous, ruthless and vengeful.[37]

Other quotes could be added, about the "terrifying murders" of which the weak, corrupt, powerless, and still-youthful Romanian democracy was guilty ("the advance of the Slavic element from the Danubian and Bessarabian regions," or the fact that "Jews have overrun the villages of Maramureş and Bukovina, and have achieved an absolute majority in all the cities of Bessarabia"[38]); there are countless other such comments, some even more ridiculous and disgusting. Absurdly infantile and aggressive as such phrases sound to us today, we must not forget that such irrationality was made legitimate at the time it was written by that simplistic, paradoxical "logic" that pretended to furnish instant solutions to long-unresolved social conflicts. This has always been the summary and deviant "logic" of extremist movements in times of crisis, as we are judiciously reminded by Lacoue-Labarthe and Nancy in their study on nazism. During the confused and oppressive period before the war, when even long-established democracies were tottering, this kind of extremist impulse unfortunately turned up in one form or another even among many intellectuals. All the more reason for extremism to have taken root in Romania, where the fragile democracy became paralyzed by internal contradictions and the complicated international situation. To that we must add the dilemmas of a long, troubled national history in which identity crises and mechanisms of easy identification with utopian ideals were fertile soil for the new extremism.

Many critics in Romania and abroad have stressed the humanist value of Eliade's literary work: the stimulating and mysterious

---

[37] Eliade, "Strigoii" ("Ghosts"), in *Cuvîntul,* January 12, 1938.
[38] Eliade, "Piloţii orbi" ("Blind Pilots"), in *Vremea,* Bucharest, September 19, 1937.

ambiguity of his prose, his magical fantasy, his enigmatic, codified reality, the free play and dreamy compassion of his writing.

Yet this does not diminish but rather aggravates the question of his involvement with fascism. Literature must meet primarily aesthetic criteria, just as scholarly work must meet scholarly standards. Writing about the case of Paul de Man, Denis Donoghue recently observed that "it would answer injustice with injustice if one were to assert that Deconstruction is compromised by de Man's wartime journalism." Journals, memoirs, and autobiographies, on the other hand, cannot endlessly avoid the ethical challenge of an examination of conscience. In fact the purpose of such works would be countered by a strategy of ambiguity, as much as if the work were limited to a narrow, conventional daily account. The Romanian literary critic Lucian Raicu has written that when a journal "hides too much, out of an excessive sense of personal dignity or modesty or the author's desire to legitimize himself morally, or for other very understandable reasons, it naturally loses all interest."

The contrast between Eliade's fiction and his militant journalism is as pronounced as the contrast between Eliade the supporter of fascism and Eliade the respected intellectual of his later years, remembered by his friends in the cordial and cosmopolitan atmosphere of his American home, where he was hospitable and affable to colleagues and acquaintances of all races and faiths. His fidelity to the spiritual values of the East and his more and more mellowed skepticism toward the West seemingly did not prevent an openness to dialogue and did not dispel the image of intellectual harmony. No one could see—and perhaps Eliade himself managed to forget—the hovering ghost of another time, another personality: the skeleton in the closet. The issues that his journals avoid persistently haunt the reader, perhaps for that very reason.

In contrast to his great predecessors, such as Eminescu, Haşdeu, and Iorga, Eliade had the "advantage" of witnessing the incomparable tragedy of the Holocaust, the unfolding of Stalinist genocide, the horrors of right- and left-wing dictatorships, and the dangerous stirrings of the Islamic fundamentalist movement. Eliade lived the greater part of his life in the West and could see that, in spite of its many shortcomings, democracy is the only system in which there can be a dialogue between the right and the left, even in their extremist forms.

We are inclined to regard sympathetically the contradictions of an intellectual, and we look for contradictions in his journals, but unfortunately we find a surprising coherence and consistency. His "happy guilt" does not refer only to his remembered adoration of Nae Ionescu.

It is hard to understand Eliade's *felix culpa.* Even harder to understand is the following entry from his autobiography: "I don't know how Corneliu Codreanu will be judged by history. The fact is that four months after the phenomenal electoral success of the Legionary movement, its head found himself sentenced to ten years at hard labor, and five months after that he was executed—events that reconfirmed my belief that our generation did not have a political destiny."[39] Codreanu was the charismatic leader of the Romanian Fascist movement; he was violently anti-Semitic and antidemocratic; he was guilty of odious murders and of political terrorism. Yet four decades after the war, Eliade appears to be uncertain about history's judgment of Codreanu, and he is still fascinated by Codreanu's electoral "success." Eliade fails to mention the murders committed by this "martyr" and does not hesitate to identify himself with that "generation" and with its political destiny. The same treatment is accorded to the Leader's lieutenants, the "martyrs" Ion Moţa and Vasile Marin, who were killed fighting with Franco's forces in January 1937. Their deaths were dramatically evoked by Eliade at the time, and he would later recall them as "models" of self-sacrifice.[40]

---

[39] Eliade, *Autobiography,* vol. 2 (Chicago: The University of Chicago Press, 1988), p. 65.
[40] Eliade, *Autobiography,* p. 65.

Ricketts informs us that the deaths of these two exemplary Legionnaires are commemorated every year in Majadahonda, Spain, and that in 1985, on the forty-eighth

As he grew older, Eliade gradually accommodated himself to the new academic and political atmosphere; he probably became less of a rebel against democracy, although it would be hard to say that he fundamentally changed his social outlook. As Seymour Cain says in his thoughtful article,

> In his autobiography Eliade never forswears his ideological association with the Legionary movement, and sees its decline and fall as a Romanian tragedy, the inevitable result of its political naiveté, rather than as a good thing. He is more like the fellow-travelers of Soviet Communism who gave up their association but never repudiated the ideology to which they had given their youthful devotion.[41]

Eliade's is probably such a case. His concept of the best social and political solution for Romania (and perhaps not only for that geographically and politically complicated area) seems to have remained constant. It is a traditional, conservative vision, skeptical of democracy and modernity, tied to ethnicity and the cultural values of the place.

Alexander Solzhenitsyn's recent call for a Slavophile Russian state comes at a time of revival of the old conflicts between the "separatists" and the "integrationists," between the supporters of independent states and the "Europeanists." In Romania this dispute was tragically manipulated during the years between the wars; now it is reemerging in a new context, pitting those who want integration into Europe against those who want to strengthen the national state and character.

---

anniversary, more than fifty Legionnaires from all over the world participated, along with 130 others. *Mircea Eliade, The Romanian Roots,* p. 1399.

[41] Seymour Cain, "Mircea Eliade, the Iron Guard, and Romanian Anti-Semitism," *Midstream,* November 1989.

The right is still no smarter than the left; it has not learned from its own disasters nor from those of the other side. Professor Katherine Verdery of Johns Hopkins University reports that, according to Constantin Noica,[42] Eliade—from his distant American home—encouraged Professor Edgar Papu to launch a debate in Romania over "protochronism."[43] Professor Papu is another sad case of an eminent Romanian who despite his scholarship is involved with an odious group of nationalist intellectuals. This debate was opened initially to emphasize the Romanian contribution to world culture. From this it gradually degenerated into an ugly ideological crusade

[42] "*Morning Star* critic Arthur Silvestri . . . had become a zealous protochronist, turning his pen to denouncing the emigré 'traitors' in Paris and Munich, calling into question the cultural representativeness of these propagators of 'pseudo-culture' and thereby invalidating their claims to cultural authority, and excommunicating its holders as 'cultural terrorists' and traitors. . . . For certain emigrés he made an exception, regarding their work as so Romanian that 'one would think it had been written here among us. . . .' These exceptions include, most visibly, world-famous *Mircea Eliade of the University of Chicago, known not only for his brilliance, not only for his association with rightist groups in the pre-Communist period, but also—as reported to me by Eliade's close friend, philosopher Constantin Noica—for his having urged Papu on to greater boldness in his protochronism.* Anti-protochronists generally regard Silvestri as a direct agent of the Romanian security police, since his column published information to which only the intelligence forces have access (the precise location of Radio Free Europe's broadcast towers, e.g.) and regularly named emigrés whose names can usually not be mentioned in print [emphasis added—N.M.]" (Katherine Verdery, *National Ideology under Socialism: Identity and Cultural Politics in Ceauşescu's Romania* [Berkeley and Los Angeles: The University of California Press, 1991 (in press)], chapter 5, p. 47).

[43] "In 1974, there appeared in the Romanian cultural publication *Twentieth Century* an article by the literary critic Edgar Papu, a scholar in his 70's. . . . His article, "Romanian Protochronism," argued that contrary to views widely held in Romania, the national literary tradition did not rest largely upon imitations of Western forms but was highly original; moreover, he said, Romanian literary creations had often anticipated creative developments in the West (such as surrealism, dadaism, etc.), even though these achievements had often not been acknowledged as such because they were little known abroad.

"The protochronist argument that began as a debate about the grounds for establishing, circulating, and accumulating literary values came to be a debate about fascism, patriotism, betrayal, and anti-Semitism.

"Even President Ceauşescu has weighed in with protochronist claims, announcing that, well before the Soviet Union and Hungary, he had had the idea of mixed or joint ventures" (Verdery, *National Ideology under Socialism,* chapter on Romanian protochronism).

similar (as I pointed out in an article actually published in Romania at the time[44]) to the period when Stalin required that the Soviet press endlessly discover new aspects of "supremacy" of Soviet over Western culture. This campaign distorted the Romanian cultural scene for some fifteen years and led to one of the most sinister manipulations and intimidations of the intelligentsia by the Ceauşescu regime. Of course the political machinators soon bridged the abyss between Eliade's thinking and their own immediate interests—which does not make his "unhappy guilt" in this casual involvement any less a responsibility, taking into account his past experiences in such matters.

Eliade mentions in the fourth volume of his journals, as in earlier ones, that he has been accused not only of "fascism," of "Nazism," but also of "anti-Semitism." It can be shown that, especially at first, Eliade associated himself with certain Jewish intellectuals and dissociated himself from the Legion's criminal "excesses." On the other hand there are enough—too many—instances in his journalism that correspond perfectly to the Legion's ideology.

Eliade's brand of nationalism appeared in his journalism in the form of anti-Hungarian and anti-Slavic babble much more than as anti-Semitism—which is hardly in his favor; quite the opposite.

Only the author could disclose the truth about himself, could explain the xenophobia that is astonishing in a scholar of his standing, especially in someone who from his first trip to India as a young man had shown himself so open to the cultural diversity of the world.

Though we can only regret Eliade's reticence regarding the bizarre and unsavory aspects of his life story, we hope that the journal of his friend Mihail Sebastian, when it is published, will fill in some of the blanks. Anyone who has read, as I have, a portion of

[44] Norman Manea, "Vocativul urgenţei" ("The Vocative of Urgency"), in *Secolul 20* 1-2-3, Bucharest, 1980.

Sebastian's journal knows that this document is essential to an understanding of pre-Holocaust Romania and Eastern Europe. Sebastian's acute, lucid, and melancholy intelligence illuminates the painful human spectacle of hate and degradation.

In its everyday, domestic aspects, the reality of "totalitarian" systems, be they Nazi, Fascist, Communist, or fundamentalist Islamic, is far more complicated than anything suggested by these labels. In practice the categories, and sometimes even the bases on which they rest, are far more complex. Honest scruples require those who have lived with postwar "true socialism" to reject simplistic recrimination, which is more likely to obfuscate than help reach an understanding of the truth. The spectacle of millions of former Party members madly reciting anti-Communist slogans is moving because it forces us to think twice before returning to our comfortable ad hoc categories. How quickly they forgot their own guilt, the unhappiness of the truly oppressed and marginalized; even the "happy" moments enjoyed during their somnolent complicity. Guilty pleasures, happy guilt? It would be hard for these past and present opportunists to admit to this kind of ambiguous happiness, just as it probably was hard for many Nazis—genuine, "convinced" Nazis who only in retrospect were forced to acknowledge the horror of the words *Nazi* and *anti-Semite,* that is, after their apocalyptic crimes were known to all—to speak of their *happy* Nazi youths, of the demonstrations, balls, lectures, and ecstatic loves that were their *felix culpa.*

Eliade's final journal is lacking the dramatic introspection that is essential to a work of this nature. Sometimes this failing is associated with and partially excused by advancing age, which occasionally produces an impression of naïveté when Eliade's tone becomes more regal than professorial (as in the long, almost imperial-style lists of conferences, dinners, audiences, and festivities held in his honor) or when it is marked, as his tone sometimes is, by an amusing narcissistic accent (for instance, he reproduces a letter from the president of the University of Chicago announcing the establishment of a Mircea Eliade Chair in the History of Religions).

An honest critical analysis of the controversial significance of Eliade's life would have justified the publication of his journals and would have had an impact on Romanian culture. Banned in Romania for the first decades after the war, Eliade began to be "retrieved" in the 1970s. This process was not without its complexities, for although on the one hand Ceauşescu's "National Stalinist" regime was striving for the kind of nationalist legitimacy the Legion had enjoyed, on the other hand the surviving leaders of the Communist old guard could not forget the political orientation of their old enemy. For instance, let's take the case of Gogu Rădulescu. It is now known that in early 1937, on learning that the left-wing student Rădulescu[45] had been detained at Legion headquarters and beaten with wet ropes, Eliade not only expressed satisfaction with this barbarous punishment but said that he himself would have put out Rădulescu's eyes.[46] When Eliade's books were being considered for publication, Rădulescu held the important position of vice president of the republic.

Nevertheless, Eliade's literary works began to be reissued and gradually some of his scholarly works appeared as well. Paradoxical, but very representative of the shady ambiguities of Ceauşescu's dictatorship, is the fact that in times of sharp atheistic propaganda, and in spite of its author's political past, *A History of Religious Ideas* was distributed to a number of "privileged" Party officials.

Eliade himself began to meet, both in the United States and

[45] Until the fall of Ceauşescu, Gogu Rădulescu was vice president of the Council of State and a member of the Executive Committee of the Romanian Communist party's Central Committee.

[46] Mihail Sebastian, *Journal.* Excerpts published in *Toladot* 1, Israel, January–March 1972; excerpts mentioned by Ricketts in his monograph.

elsewhere, not only with Romanian writers but with Romanian "officials," even with representatives of the government.[47] When he mentions these meetings in the journals he sometimes uses a system of codes; this is perhaps understandable in a person who has always been attracted to magic and ritual, to the effects of masks and secrecy. For instance, in connection with the donation of part of his library to Romania he mentions the Romanian ambassador, Mircea Maliţa, Gheorghe Folescu, the commercial attaché at the Romanian embassy, Folescu's wife, and even someone named Adrian. On the other hand, the person who helped Eliade's sister retrieve an old icon from their parents' house with the assistance of the Romania Association, an organization through which the Romanian government maintains "cultural contact" with emigrants, is mentioned only by the initials V.C. Could this be a form of protection for the person who risked an "illegal" act? If so, why give the initials? The Romanian reader may well be able to divine the name of Virgil Cândea, the "Party charge" at the Romania Association, a learned scholar and official "cultural agent" who was coerced into various dubious missions during the last decade of the Ceauşescu dictatorship.

Eliade's political past could not be discussed in Romania, but his work was so highly respected and his personality so fascinating that his name gradually made its way into many publications and into the concerns of many intellectuals. His name was also used by the very noisy new nationalists in several journals (*Săptămîna, Luceafărul, Flacăra*) that enjoyed the protection of and were even encouraged by the authorities.

In 1982, a particularly black year in Ceauşescu's leftist-rightist dictatorship, I saw *Iphigenia* at the National Theater in Bucharest. This play by Eliade was first performed in 1941, another dark Fascist year, and was reissued in 1951, in Romanian, by a right-wing expatriate in Argentina.[48] As in 1941, no doubt, the tension outside

[47] Eliade, *Journal IV,* pp. 48, 77, 80, 81, 86.
[48] Ricketts, *Mircea Eliade, The Romanian Roots,* p. 1449.

the theater and the mood of the audience—fear, disgust, exhaustion, and despair—interacted with the play in a most unfortunate way, so that it had the effect of a kind of exaltation of death for a glorious "cause," a joyous and transcendent sacrifice. I was reminded of a comment in Sebastian's journal regarding the 1941 performance of this play: "Voices that cry out, that shout, false declamatory gestures . . ."[49]

In Romania, after fifty years of censorship from both the left and the right, little is known about Eliade that is accurate. In the final years before Ceauşescu's fall, the Romanian dissident Dan Petrescu wrote, in an essay smuggled to the West, that "a campaign is beginning in the West to unmask Mircea Eliade's ties to the extreme right during the period between the wars. This may at least lead, as it did for Heidegger, to increased popularity for his work."[50]

At issue is not the popularity of Eliade's work as a cause célèbre; nor can he be considered unknown in the West, judging by the list of his publications. As for the questions raised by his life, a debate should have taken place long ago in Romania itself, where it is of immeasurable importance. It is difficult to say whether, even in the post-Ceauşescu era, a debate of this kind will find a sufficiently objective climate in which to take place.

Petrescu went on to say, "If the collaboration of Romanian intellectuals with the present regime—which is anything but leftist—were to be discussed one day, then we'll have a show!" This is certainly true. Not only was Ceauşescu's regime anything but leftist, but the same was true of the members (about four million of them!) of the Communist party, who could hardly have been considered Communist, since in Romania the political orientation was to the right. Petrescu wrote these lines during Ceauşescu's last days.

[49] Mihail Sebastian, *Journal.*
[50] Dan Petrescu and Liviu Cangeopol, "Ce-ar mai fi de spus? (Convorbiri libere într-o ţară ocupată)" ("What More Can You Say? Free Conversations in an Occupied Country"), in *Agora,* February 1990, Foreign Policy Research Institute, Philadelphia, p. 213.

Now that show is on, and it is often grotesque. Everyone cries out his own innocence, his own suffering. Some of the loudest voices come from the former "intellectual" servants of the dictatorship. . . . The problems with the democratization process bring to mind the country's complicated history, with identity crises and mechanisms of easy identification again working together to prolong the posttotalitarian impasse.

A terrible show indeed! In the rush to the new opportunism, unmasking campaigns have, naturally, a violently anti-Communist character. What is amusing is the fact that no one, it seems, had anything to do with that black operetta in which so many played a role with zeal and verve and profit.

Some encouraging effects of the transition to democracy can, however, be seen. Less than two months after Ceauşescu's disappearance, the brave young critic Dan C. Mihăilescu wrote the following in the literary review *România Literară:*

> For decades intellectual Romania of the period between the wars was viewed with all kinds of prejudices. These prejudices must be defused and dismantled with care, with delicate firmness as it were. Over Eliade, over the entire generation of '27, . . . hangs the black cloud of the right-wing Legion. It is time for us to blow hard, not to remove it (logically and practically, that is impossible), but to move it aside for a while so that we can see things in the light of day. We have no true and all-encompassing text for the Thirties, neither for the Left nor the Right. . . .

The critic invites objective research, "free from obsessions," into Eliade's work and personality. He adds, with the same clear-eyed fairness, "Eliade too, like the rest of his generation, cannot but be *y compris* in this period, with all its aggravating or extenuating circumstances—*all of them.*"[51]

The time may be coming when the Legion period, and the

---

[51] Dan C. Mihăilescu, "Mircea Eliade, 'Made in USA,' " in *România Literară,* February 15, 1990.

Communist one, can be analyzed clearly. If in Romania today there can be open and lengthy discussion of great writers like Mihail Sadoveanu, George Călinescu, Tudor Arghezi, and Camil Petrescu and their compromises with the Communist regime (a dictatorship that from the start was not easy to oppose), would it not also be appropriate to analyze the voluntary involvement ("happy guilt"), with all its consequences, of Eliade and other writers and intellectuals in the right-wing movement? This is all the more important now that communism is no longer a real threat in Romania. In a sense, indeed, it never was. Ceauşescu's Stalinism gradually became a camouflaged fascism. The forces of totalitarianism are still strong and by no means ready to surrender; their true motivation is not necessarily ideological, more likely practical.

Another truly important text came out during this post-totalitarian spring, "Separating from Eminescianism," written by Virgil Nemoianu of the Catholic University in Washington.[52] Skillfully analyzing the legacy of Mihai Eminescu's ideas as reflected in Romanian thought and behavior during the last century, the author proposes a clear, critical look at "the sabotaging of history," at the rejection of Western democracy and modernity, and at nationalistic isolationism with all its excesses as seen in the philosophy of Pârvan, Goga, Haşdeu, Iorga, Vulcănescu, Eliade, and Noica. Nemoianu stresses the fact that in Romania "there is a steep slope from the highest levels of philosophical debate to the lowest, polarizations quickly become coarse and menacing and tend toward the nationalistic right, the totalitarian left, or even the frivolous and grasping center." In this context, continues Nemoianu, "the Byzantine, neo-Platonic sources of Romanian culture (with their emphatic separation between faith and human action)" can only lead to stagnation; he therefore argues for "parting ways with Eminescu" and with "post-Eminescianism" in favor of a realistic, objective, rational approach to social change.

---

[52] Virgil Nemoianu, "Despărţirea de eminescianism" ("Separating from Eminescianism"), in *Caiet de literatură*, supplement to *Dialog*, May 1990, pp. 14–18.

We must hope that this salutary call will have favorable echoes. The collapse of the bankrupt totalitarian "left" has much to teach the "right," whether disguised in cynical conservatism or bursting out in bloody nationalist rituals.

Romania means more than just Ceauşescu or Codreanu, more even than the green-shirted terrorists of the Legion or the uniforms of the Securitate. Romania also has a legacy of democratic thought, albeit weak and stifled for many decades by right- and left-wing dictators. There is a Romanian sense of humor and a Romanian common sense; there is also an undeniably deep relationship with European culture. And there are Romanian paradoxes and ambiguities that have not always been detrimental to its destiny. We might mention that, in a country with traditions of anti-Semitism, still many Jews were allowed to survive during World War II.

Hope should not reside in paradox and ambiguity, but in a future that will see a clear, unambiguous transition to a civil society.

> Bard College,
> September 1990
> *Translated by Alexandra Bley-Vroman*

POSTSCRIPTUM

Since the writing of this essay, many ugly events have transpired that reveal the lasting legacies of Romania's nationalist, fascist, and communist past. In the Romanian nationalist press, Mircea Eliade, Nae Ionescu, and other right-wing Romanian thinkers have been canonized. If that weren't scandalous enough, there has been an official rehabilitation of Ion Antonescu, Hitler's ally.

Offsetting these ignominious episodes have been some very serious debates in the democratic press on the lasting guilt of the right-wing fascist intellectuals. (Especially notable is an article by Alexandru George aptly entitled "White Bolshevism.")

At this sad juncture what conclusions can be drawn? Perhaps it is still appropriate to hope, even fantasize, that were Eliade alive and aware of these events, he would now side with the angels and commit himself to a true civil society.

Bard College
July 1991

THE HISTORY OF
AN INTERVIEW

In the summer of 1985 I received a phone call from a Securitate officer, who identified himself as a captain in the Ministry of the Interior and asked to see me. At my insistence he hinted that it was about "an application. . . ."

He allowed me to choose the place, and I suggested my apartment. Recently I had been impressed by a writer friend who had gone through such a "meeting" and had requested that small privilege. Naturally I would feel more confident in my own room than in any place my "guest" might suggest. Naively, I thought that from the very outset I had won some slight acknowledgment of my dignity. The meeting was set for the next morning at nine.

Yes, months before I had applied for a passport to go to France and Germany as a tourist. I supposed that was the application he was referring to. My first trip to Western Europe, in 1979, had been approved after many rejections. That first visit to the West at the age of forty-three had been terribly unsettling. The hopeless return had upset me even more, bringing on an extended period of depression. I had decided not to repeat this experience too soon, knowing that after a few weeks of exhilaration I would plunge once more into a prolonged state of paralyzing apathy and neurosis. For six years I had not applied for another passport, but by 1985 a feeling of suffocation had become intolerable: I urgently needed to get out of my cage, however briefly.

After that disturbing telephone conversation, I tried to reassure myself; if the Securitate officer had in fact called to discuss my travel application, then the morning's meeting would be fairly routine, *pro forma:* at my repeated questioning, the president of the Writers' Union had given me to understand that this passport matter had been settled in my favor.

I had special cause to feel ill at ease at any sign from that dreaded Institution, even taking into consideration the tension shared by everyone detained in the "multilaterally developed" camp of Ceauşescu's Romania, and the peculiar status that my occupation and my ethnic background put me in. Ten years earlier a close friend of mine had been pressured into becoming an informer, his only duty being to report on me. I remembered well that damp and smoky fall evening when he called me from a public phone and suggested that we go for a walk. Nothing in his voice would have given me an indication of what was to follow. He had come straight from an appointment with the Securitate. It had not taken very much persuading: they had insinuated that he might lose his modest job and be unable to support his sick father. And so he had signed the "contract" and was even given a code name. Once or even twice a week, in various private apartments around Bucharest, he was to meet his contact officer to discuss me, to answer questions, and to draft what the Securitate called "informational notes."

It would be hard to forget the anxiety and fear that engulfed us both, or my odd feeling of estrangement from and, paradoxically, closeness to him.

Our relationship took on an increasingly obvious and schizophrenic urgency. I became addicted to our exchanges. He reported on his meetings with his contact; he described the shabby apartments where they met, the examiner's appearance and reactions, the questions and the answers. I insisted on more and more details; I overwhelmed him with demands for new explanations to questions he had already answered (in the event they should arise in subsequent talks). As my need to see him grew, I wanted to know every detail of these "informational" meetings, and yet I became increasingly hesitant to share with him even the ordinary trivia of my daily life. More and more suspicious, I developed less and less faith in his always prompt reports. I started to think that he was hiding some things from me, to protect me—and himself. My life simply was not spectacular enough to warrant so many meetings and such constant surveillance. What could there have been to discuss at such great length about my rather ordinary family, my friends, projects, foreign connections, income, health, books, even women?

Two years after the start of his schizophrenic role, my friend emigrated from Romania. After his departure, no one else confessed to this role, but undoubtedly he had been replaced, probably by someone close to me. . . .

Tangled memories and doubts held sleep at bay on the night before the appointment. How much did they know? What would they ask? In moments like this you try to recall conversations with friends, hazily remembered events, as well as letters or telephone conversations or secrets that could be exploited by "them."

A little before nine I began to listen for the elevator, but I didn't hear a sound. At nine my doorbell rang. I opened the door: a young man, tall, slim, blond; gray suit, blue shirt, tie. Clearly he had come up the stairs. According to the scenario I had planned, I asked to see his identification. He gave me a piercing look and smiled condescendingly. He flicked up an I.D. card, but I did not have time to see the picture or the name before it disappeared into the juggler's pocket.

He was already in the room. He looked around at the shelves of books, the desk, at his tired host in sweater and jeans.

"Do you have a needle and thread?"

The first part of our duet had already been fairly unusual: the examinee had solemnly requested the examiner's identification, but before he could adjust his glasses on his nose, the man on stilts had swallowed it up, poof, as if by magic. The second part was even more promising: it seemed to be based on that French comedy with Patachon, the short fat guy, and Pat, the tall thin guy. Here were Patachon, the quarry, the plump author in slippers, and Pat, the elegant hunter—new additions to the traditional repertory of the genre—with a little number called "Forever Human." Upon walking in he looked at the pale and rather odd gentleman and remarked warmly, "You know, you look like my father. . . ." The hunter delicately pretended not to see the quarry's consternation. Instead he eyed the shelves of books with interest. I did not move.

"A button popped off my pants as I was running up the stairs," the captain said. He showed me the button, then pointed to the fly, to the place of the missing, problematic Securitate button. Had he pulled it off so that he could be alone in the room for a moment? How could he have known I did not have needle and thread right there, that I would have to leave the room? And why? Did he want to install a bug to replace my friend who had abandoned his post? I had fallen into the trap they loved so well, paranoia. If they wanted to install something they could do it anytime. Would it be better to accept the farce that things were what they seemed? To do somersaults and walk on a tightrope? I returned his boyish grin with a fatherly smile. We both smiled, humanized, with shared hypocritical compassion.

I spent a long time in the bedroom hunting unhurriedly for the sewing kit. At last, according to script, I presented it to him, letting him choose the poisoned needle and the magic thread. The young man was sitting shyly in an armchair, and shyly began to sew up that shameful spot, observed with shy suspicion by his older companion. This conspiratorial little scene was played out slowly, as it must be.

"Are you still angry?" The words came softly.

I waited until he finished sewing, to see whether he would fill in some details so that I could understand the question.

"That interview a few years back. . . . The interview there was all that hoopla about. Are you still angry?"

No, I must confess I had not anticipated this question either. I must admit the scenario I had envisioned during the night did not include this. I should have paused to prepare a careful answer, but I came back at once, "Yes, very angry."

I had not intended to make a serious reply. In the very interview he referred to I had said that we must not "dignify" officialdom with a somber attitude, that by "taking it . . . seriously, and inadvertently reinforcing its authority, [we would be] acknowledging that authority." But I could not hold myself in check. I had not forgotten that business. Nor, apparently, had those who kept me under surveillance and who directed the show from the wings.

In the summer of 1981, four years earlier, just after the Writers' Conference, I had been interviewed by an important literary critic. The conference was an unprecedented demonstration against official cultural policy and against official policy itself. The speeches were never published. Not even the delegates were allowed to carry tape recorders into the conference hall, lest there be any "evidence" of what was being said. Unruly clowns, we were locked up for three days in an elegant hall, where we were allowed to frolic while the surveillance team took down the names of the most daring and recorded for the Institution's files the naive battle cries, the bursts of laughter, the whistles, the frenzy, the impertinence, and the unforgettable jubilation of our childish get-together.

Apparently Ceauşescu had had a speaker installed in his office to hear the speeches from the auditorium. It was the first time that the secretary general of the Party was not in attendance at an event like this. That morning groups of Young Pioneers had been standing in front of the hall, ready to cheer him and present him with flowers, when suddenly the ceremony was cancelled.

The president's last-minute decision to stay away from the Writers' Conference (obviously based on Securitate information regarding the mood of the delegates) was a wise one. While delivering his tedious address, his replacement, Prime Minister Dăscălescu, noticed with dismay that the insolent writers were leaving the hall one by one to smoke in the corridor or to stuff themselves at the abundant buffet laden with delicacies unavailable to ordinary mortals. "Real hot dogs!" a friend of mine exclaimed, delighted. "Real hot dogs! They really taste like hot dogs, not like those disgusting artificial ones we get in the store. Hot dogs, hot dogs, incredible, fantastic, like in the fifties!" My greedy friend was overjoyed, hardly dreaming that he was soon to be deprived not only of the pleasure of hot dogs, real or artificial, but of his life, happy or unhappy as it might have been.

Exasperation had reached unprecedented levels, but this was only one explanation for the atmosphere at this conference (one of the most violent anti-Communist demonstrations in Eastern Europe of that period, I think); the other was the composition of the audience. For the first time delegates had been elected by secret ballot. As a result, the nationalistic faction of the official writers, personae gratae of the Powers That Be, were not present. Deeply displeased, the authorities subsequently retaliated by unleashing a new round of intimidations: they tightened censorship, reduced funds, decreased the size of print runs, paralyzed the Writers' Union, prohibited contact with foreigners, and stepped up the persecution of "unmanageable" writers.

The interview with the literary critic took place immediately after the conference but did not appear in print until six months later. (A transcript of the interview follows this essay, on p. 168.) It came out in *Familia,* a good cultural journal of limited circulation issued in Oradea, far from the capital. It was somewhat easier to get a relatively normal piece published in the provinces, especially in Transylvania, where comparison with the freer press of nearby Hungary seems to have restrained the censors at times. But the content and the name of the person interviewed aroused the prompt fury of the authorities. A smear campaign was launched, ostensibly against the substance of the interview but actually to vilify the subject. It is a tried-and-true debating tactic not to address an undesirable opinion but to attack the person who expresses it.

The literary columnist of the official nationalist faction wrote that he had "never heard of this author's name." A strange bit of false modesty for this critic, who in many of his articles between 1969 and 1973 (before what I call the "hit squad" had been formed) had mentioned my name and included me among the most important contemporary writers, although at the time I had published only two books. In another and somewhat similar instance, early in the smear campaign the official poet of the Penal Court (and Colony), Adrian Păunescu, took personal umbrage at my reference to "a new Mayakovsky, a new Alexandru Toma," and wrote that "Norman Manea . . . has not come to my attention until now, nor has his work." Years later a writer with ties to the Bucharest literary scene told me that the "court poet" was quite familiar with at least one of my novels and that he had recognized himself in a rather unsympathetic minor character, to whom indeed he did bear a certain resemblance.

The campaign against me typically employed a broader, more "expressive" spectrum of invective: "liberaloid," "outsider," "Stalinist," "of another language and of another faith," "anti-Party." These contradictory labels were hastily mixed together and no one could stop, contest, or silence the carnival of outrage and fury unleashed by the country's premier Institution that supported and paid for this tirade.

My conversation with the Securitate officer had lasted almost two hours and we were still on the same subject.

"If you're still angry, that means they've achieved their goal," my young opponent in this game of cat and mouse had pressed, the button sequence having been brought to a spirited finish.

"Who are 'they'?" I asked.

"The ones who were attacking you," he answered too logically.

Childishly I took up the old man's role again. "I'm not angry with them. It was their right, even their job to attack me. I'm angry because I was not allowed to reply. I wrote to the Central Committee of the Communist party and they never even acknowledged my letter, though the law requires that they reply to any communication from the public within sixty days."

The clever officer smiled. "A form letter? You would have been satisfied with a form letter?" He had obviously learned how to pose questions at the Institution. Yes, the examinee would have been satisfied with a form letter, he even admitted it.

"I'm not so dumb, you know, I wasn't expecting anything else. I'm not looking for justice, or waiting for an apology, God knows. Yes, a form letter, that's all I was waiting for! A form letter: 'Your registered letter number such and such was received on such and such a date and the points raised in it will be looked into.' That's all. That's all!" The host had risen to his feet to put more feeling into his solo. The visitor smiled again. There would have been no point in sending a form letter. A concrete, efficient reply, yes, that would have meant something! . . . And where *was* this efficient reply? The rattled victim was ready to cry out and then collapse in the arms of the beast. Those words, however, would have been too spontaneous and my reaction too genuine.

The room quivered with suspense. There was a long, tense wait before the officer gained control of his mask and voice and delivered these solemn lines: "You had your answer from the highest authority in the land. Comrade Ceauşescu, president of the country and secretary general of the Party, spoke very firmly against nationalism at the last Union Congress."

Oh yes, of course, the Highest Authority!

After this pronouncement we observed an obligatory moment of silence and reflection, neither cat nor mouse daring to crack a smile or a joke. Only after that could the first faint rustling of the Mouse be heard. . . . If the Highest Authority . . . if the Great . . . well then, why . . . why?

"Then why are nationalist, anti-intellectual, anti-Semitic, and anti-Western texts still being printed?" I asked, with no hint of a smile.

Tomcat sighed wearily, like a retired policeman. He remained silent, waiting, as in a classic scene, to see tears smear the clown's makeup as he is moved by his oppressor's kindness.

It became clear that the officer was from the Department of Minorities. I might have considered this choice an insult if I had not remembered all too well my meeting with the much more dangerous and clever officer from the Department of Literature, whose cold and sly approach lingered in my memory. Evidently the Institution regarded my reference to the chauvinism of the dictator's party as the most incriminating comment in the scandalous interview, which was the first time anyone had protested publicly against "Ideals," a neo-Fascist editorial published in the journal *Săptămîna* (*The Week*) in 1980.

It had been difficult to take that step. Under the totalitarian regime of Romania in the eighties, when the entire population suffered intolerable poverty, moral filth, and terror, it seemed "indecent" to single out nationalism as the single target of criticism. In the end I decided to put aside my reticence, because the use of nationalism to distract the population was a sign of the rapidly mounting disaster. I had hoped that there would be a reaction to the article from someone other than a member of the minority. . . .

The officer gave me time to think back. I had no trouble in recalling the emphatic, abject lines in "Ideals": "We owe no one an accounting of what we do; we are free, we are the majority, and we are the masters in our own country; millions of loyal sons of this country have made the historic choice of Romanian-style communism." (The irony of placing the words "the majority" alongside the words "free" and "masters" was no doubt involuntary.) The point of the fascistic manifesto was swiftly, inexorably made:

> We, the writers and artists of Romania in these heroic times, love the Communist party not only for the fresh, new vision that it has brought to the evolution of Romanian society as a whole, not only for the electrifying rhythm in which it is going forward toward the general good, toward quality and optimization, but in equal measure for the truly revolutionary courage with which it holds that Romania as a nation can only be built by the people of this land, people born here hundreds and thousands of years ago, who do not desert the battle when times are tough.

The Party knew all this, of course, and much more, but revealed it only rarely and then only to its faithful servants! The article actually continued,

> The Party knows all this and more . . . this represents the basis for the selection and promotion of its members. It knows, for instance, that the highest honors must be accorded to those who *perform patriotic deeds,* as the ancient chronicler said, and not to money-hungry visitors, to teachers of the democratic tarantella in their smelly old alpacas, to racketeers whose interests are foreign to those of this nation, who jingle their arrogance in their pockets and fool some people with their fake patriotism. We need no lazy prophets, no Judases in whose cheap and venal blood the heritage of Romanian sacrifice does not flow.

"Prophets and Judases," "democratic tarantella," "racketeers with foreign interests," "fakes," "venal blood," I repeated to myself as I replied to the questions in that hazardous interview. . . . It had long been apparent that the Party was ridding its ranks of "foreigners," of citizens who had not lived in the country for "hundreds and thousands of years." The use of expressions such as "teachers of the democratic tarantella," "lazy prophets," and "Judases" showed that the expulsion of undesirables had now become an urgent priority. Those at the top of the blacklist must be not only excluded from the "highest honors" but provoked and driven out. In this manner, two of the Conducător's great goals would be achieved: "purification of the people" and acquisition of hard currency in exchange for these contaminated foreigners, who must be segregated from "the people of this land." Thus Jews were sold to Israel, Germans to West Germany.

This editorial was basic to an understanding of the "membership selection policy," that is, of Ceauşescu's Party policy, and it had never been more clearly or more impudently expressed than in *Săptămîna,* the "cultural organ" of the Securitate. To attack it was blasphemy, needless to say. Any other insolence in my interview faded beside this. . . .

I looked up. My guest was relaxed, smiling. Was this a sign that the conversation had entered a new stage? Would the Securitate man now switch to a confessional, complicitous tone? Was that how he had planned Part Two of the scenario? Yes, sure . . . he was pained by many of the deficiencies of the society that he controlled. Yes, yes, the officer had his troubles too. But what about those who had publicly attacked me even after the Great Leader had given his Great Answer at the Great Congress? Why they, they are just a bunch of troublemakers. That's the word the officer used: troublemakers. Troublemakers? Past and future members of the Central Committee, present and future members of the Romanian Academy, bearers of titles and prizes and passports—troublemakers? Yes, a bunch of troublemakers, my competent examiner confirmed with a pained expression. Here was something we agreed on!

"We know about their dirty business dealings, the fortunes they've built up. They're a bunch of thugs, good-for-nothings, a bunch of troublemakers, don't pay any attention to them. Let me tell you, they don't represent the Party line. The Party dissociates itself from undignified business like that."

But the facts are that they praise the Party and the Party praises them, and their publications are edited and approved by the Party! *Săptămîna* is the house organ of the Committee for Socialist Culture and Education for the Party Municipality of Bucharest—doesn't it represent the Party? And if *Săptămîna* does not represent the Party and if the Party dissociates itself from the devotion with which it serves and uses the Party cause, then why does the Party not fire the editors of this journal and put in someone who does represent the "true" Party line? And why are you telling me all this? Should I change places with these devoted card-carrying Party employees? Me, the Mouse, not even a Party member, in fact alleged to be anti-Party? I'm supposed not even to know the language of the country where I live and am cursed!

The Securitate officer gave another long sigh. "Things are much more complicated than you realize. You shouldn't be mixed up in this kind of mess. You're a European type. . . ."

I opened my eyes and ears wide: was he being ironic? It sounded as though the Cat was trying to whistle like the bird he had just swallowed. I suddenly remembered a Soviet writer who often came to Romania: he had told me that each time he returned to Moscow he always had to report on the *Party intellectuals* to the head of the Romanian Section of the Soviet Central Committee. When the apparatchik was told that the Party intellectuals were nationalists he breathed easily. "It's all right then. The Romanian, Bulgarian, and Hungarian nationalists will never come to any agreement. I was afraid they might be Europeans. There are Europeans all over now, and I thought there might be some in Romania. The Europeans are the really dangerous ones. . . ."

"Yes, you are a fine and respected writer. A European type, a civilized person. You shouldn't bother with jerks. Your attackers have done us a lot of harm, a whole lot of harm. I don't know whether you see the foreign papers, but these irresponsible people have done the country great damage, they've jeopardized Romania's prestige in the world."

Of course they had, and they were still doing it. Then why do you pay them, and for how much longer? Once again I almost asked the double-edged questions to match his double-edged answers. But I controlled myself: it would be rude to disturb this delicate moment of confession. But another long, ambiguous silence fell, and then the officer came straight to the point.

"Why don't you emigrate?" He put it diffidently.

"Is that a suggestion?" The examinee answered a question with a question, in the manner of his people.

"Not at all," the Cat quickly retorted. Assuring me again how well respected I was, and so on and so forth. The officer stood up, and up and up, looming up to the ceiling.

In the corridor Pat and Patachon exchanged half-smiles as they had at the beginning of their duet.

"You'll get your passport soon," the officer concluded, doing up his jacket buttons and checking that all of them were in place.

Was he just sent to placate me, so that I would leave this country that I did not want to abandon with a better impression of it? "I know. Months ago, the president of the Writers' Union told me that it had been settled." Tiredly I put in my parting comment.

"The president of your union doesn't give out passports. We give out the passports," he retorted firmly, dismissively, his hand on the doorknob.

The Securitate officer's naive attempt to "calm" me was not in the least reassuring. I saw now that the Institution was obsessed with this issue and that my file was growing. But it was only in 1990 that I found out what had really happened at the official level as a result of my *Familia* interview. A fellow suspect, Radu Enescu, assistant editor of *Familia* at the time of the interview's publication, in the spring of 1990 revealed in a journal that the interview had become a "state problem." One of the brightest cultural figures in Romania, he had courageously published the interview, and had borne the consequences discreetly and with dignity.

The Securitate man's hypocritical deprecation of the Institution's cultural "troublemakers" would not have fooled even a child. It was perfectly true, as he said, that he knew all about their dirty "business dealings." But it was not just a matter of the material advantages or the immunity that the Securitate's cultural hit squad enjoyed. It was a matter of their real dirty dealings: plagiarism, ghostwritten books, connivance, abuse of power. . . . It is not an accident that all this was overlooked by the authorities: much of this is yet to be uncovered to this day.

Not long before the officer's visit, the tragicomic hand of chance—something the Securitate did not fully control—had cast some light on an aspect of the sinister masquerade. Not far from Bucharest, at the stadium in Ploieşti, a series of performances were held at which some poems dedicated to the beloved Conducător were performed to rock music. The program, called the Flacăra Club after the journal edited by Adrian Păunescu, was run by our official poet. During one wild performance, part of the stands collapsed. When thousands of hysterical teenagers fled their seats, they left behind interesting tokens of the patriotic spirit of these orgiastic, fascistic shows: bras and panties, vodka, wine, beer, and champagne bottles, more panties, bras, and condoms. It was an embarrassment for the organizer, Presidential Poet Păunescu, who had been using the Flacăra Club to build up both his political and pecuniary capital. The scandal that followed naturally brightened the star of his rival, the younger patriotic poet Corneliu Vadim Tudor.

In 1990, after the dictator's death, a document was made public that revealed the true character of the Securitate's "cultural" agents. This document was the letter Păunescu had addressed to President Ceauşescu on the day he was dismissed as editor of *Flacăra* following the accident in Ploieşti. It was dated Monday, July 8, 1985, the same week I was visited by the officer with the defective button. The text bears reproducing:

Good and beloved Leader of the Romanians, Comrade Nicolae Ceauşescu:
   I write to you these lines, disturbing you once again, because it is my impression now as so often in the past, that I am addressing justice and goodness themselves in human form. After weeks and weeks of agony I have been summoned and informed that I have been dismissed. I left Party headquarters in a daze.
   I do not wish to annoy you by repeating that the unfortunate incident in Ploieşti, which I will never cease to regret, has been used to remove a reliable defender of the "Ceauşescu Doctrine" from the field of battle. I will not even say that I am completely innocent, that I am guilty of no errors or mistakes; but my errors, crimes, mistakes, which I do recognize and regret, are not the ones of which I have been accused, and have nothing to do with the reasons for which I was dismissed from *Flacăra*. I simply wish to say that if this is your decision, it can only be a just one. I have faith in your genius and in your fairness. I realize that no one can stop the machinery that has been set in motion and that promises to deprive me of everything. The purpose of this letter is only to close one of life's

chapters, perhaps in my case to close life itself, by expressing to you my deep gratitude for having given me such opportunities for cultural activity, development, and expression, as few intellectuals have had the good fortune to enjoy. I earnestly beg you to believe that all the good I may have done I did because I believed in my Country and in You, and that any harm I may have done I did with no ill will.

Now I am no one. Now anyone can trample my life, my former work, my name in the dirt. I am ruined. I know how many enemies have been waiting for this moment.

All that is left to me is my love for my people and my Country, my duty to my children and to my poor father who has just suffered a stroke. . . . And I carry with me, to sustain me on the long, empty road, my boundless faith in You, the supreme guarantor of the good of us all, my love for everything You do at the helm of our national destiny, and the devotion I owe You always. The feelings I have nurtured for You I still nurture, and I will do so all my life. I loved You when I was editor-in-chief, and not because I was somebody— now that I am nobody, I love You as much. And if You should ever need me, and if I am still living and have the strength to rise up out of my hopelessness and suffering, with my last strength I would kneel and bend my head if that were necessary to enable the Man of Our Country to mount into the saddle of the Lord of Our Freedom, Dignity, and Survival; I would bow down to raise You as high as possible, ready for any battle, for You are the Good and Fearless and Wonderful Man!

Long live Romania! Long live the spirit of the Ninth Congress of the Romanian Communist party! Long live Nicolae Ceauşescu! A name of a Man, a heart of Valor, a title of a chapter in the Modern History of Romania! Long live the genius who knows, has always known, and will always know right from wrong and faithful soldiers from disguised traitors!

Thank You for everything—I am only sorry that I could not do more, do better, be more efficient.

Long life to You! Although I have been brought so low I can freely say that if some villain should threaten your life, I stand ready to shield your chest. It is at moments like these that one sees a man's true character. I would rather die a man of character than live a coward.

In spite of pumping out thousands of laudatory and flattering words, the author of this letter did not protect the dictator with his own chest, as he promised. In December 1989, during the uprising in Bucharest, attacked by an angry mob, the poet tried to find refuge in the American embassy with a briefcase full of jewels, we are told. Then he disappeared for a while. At present he is once more at the center of public life in Romania.

The lines I have quoted at such tedious length were emblematic not only of a period but of a profession, *the profession of self-abasement:* this was taken up voluntarily (not under duress as in the Stalinist period) and practiced with zeal in various ways both under the dictator and afterward. Whether skillfully or not, it is always done cunningly, shamelessly, and for profit. A profession representative of a world of farce where the devil, a traveling salesman peddling souls in exchange for small rewards, is a cheap swindler. But these shady strategies are always dangerous, always poisonous. The inventive cynicism of these professional mummers contrasts with the exhaustion, nausea, and complicity of the numbed and oppressed population (the "disgust syndrome," as I called it in a short story).

The hit squad was not synonymous with the "Party intellectuals," but it was a special guard. Its members owed unconditional loyalty to the Conducător and his Securitate rather than to the Party. The hit squad was also distinct from the elite nomenklatura with which it worked at times (like any terrorist group), although it despised it. This select group was allowed "freedoms" forbidden to the Party hierarchy and often enjoyed greater privileges. The Marxist makeup it wore on festive occasions could not hide the impatient nationalism that burst out from it regularly.

The weapons the hit squad used were denunciation, defamation, and diversionary tactics. There were other targets, real or invented, but "foreigners," "liberals," "cosmopolitans," or "European types" were the preferred ones. Occasionally, when it suited the stage directors in uniform, attacks on certain official organizations were permitted: for example the Writers' Union was accused of "elitism," of "syndicalism," and even "professionalism," and there had been a call for the establishment of a Party Writers' Union. The very fact that there could be a category of "writers of pro-Party patriotic poetry and prose" shows the Byzantine character of this post-Stalinist, post-Nazi (possibly even postmodern?) dictatorship, with its manipulated, interwoven, and encoded connotations.

The hit squad played an important role in the cultural program of Ceauşescu's dictatorship. A case in point was the extended official campaign favoring "protochronism," which asserts the supremacy of Romanian cultural values, over "synchronism," which views national values in a general context of world culture. The dictatorship used this debate as an ongoing weapon for intimidating the intelligentsia. (There was also an allusion to the "proto-synchro" debate in my interview.)

Perhaps I should focus on just four members of this hit squad, representative of the Ceauşescu regime and, unfortunately, also of the first year of the post-Ceauşescu period:

- Eugen Barbu—corresponding member of the Academy and several times a member of the Central Committee of the Romanian Communist party, "Socialist Boss" of *Săptămîna;* writer of sketchy and picturesque prose (and accused of plagiarism more than once); nationalist and scandal-monging journalist. We could call him "the Boss."

- Adrian Păunescu—a not-untalented poet, so prolific as to trivialize himself, ceaselessly pumping out words of praise, despair, remorse, and fear; an impetuous and demagogic journalist; editor-in-chief of *Flacăra* (and director of the Flacăra Club); an ardent and well-paid supporter of the Conducător. Let us give him the code name "the Lyric Pump."

- Corneliu Vadim Tudor—a patriotic rhymester; a journalistic hired gun; a protégé of the Boss, competing with the Lyric Pump

for the post of Poet of the Ceauşescu Dynasty. Famous for his
nationalist, Fascist-hued writings (including his unsigned editorial "Ideals" in *Săptămîna*). Let's use his first name, "Corneliu."
- Ille Purcaru—a journalist of Mafia-like efficiency obsessed
with nationalism; he carried out perfectly planned missions,
throwing off his enemies by using his true face as a mask. Let
us call him, delicately, "Anonymous."

Ridiculous as they are, these are not minor figures nor harmless
ones. They are fixed points in the nationalist-Stalinist dictatorship
that ruled Romania for the last decades. They played a role in the
smear campaign that followed the publication of the interview—a
minor episode, one might say, in their careers. But it was significant
precisely because it illustrates how things were done even in this
rather unspectacular case (one that did not include arrest, torture,
or murder), and reveals the nature of the system and of those who
served it. The profession of self-abasement was essential to the
maintenance of the dictatorship. Unfortunately, it still represents a
danger even after the dictator's death. In this sense the modest
history of an interview reflects History itself.

The interview that took place in the summer of 1981 was published
in December of that year. The first official reaction was not unexpected. It appeared in the Boss's journal, *Săptămîna*, of course,
which was overseen by the Bucharest Committee for Socialist
Culture and Education—that is, the Party. *Săptămîna* often published "special pieces": excerpts from private journals confiscated
by the Securitate, compromising political information from the
Institution's files, violent attacks on foreign "enemies" and on
"imperialist" radio stations (Radio Free Europe, Voice of America,
the BBC, etc.).

To begin with, the Institution's "professionals" wrote a short
piece in a sober tone and a concentrated style that appeared under
the headline "Bewildered" in mid-January 1982.

The publication in *Familia* of an interview with Norman Manea, which also includes some remarks about our journal, is regrettable. We would like to remind *Familia* and the subject of that interview that, with regard to the matter Norman Manea raised again after so long, *Săptămîna* has already acknowledged on two occasions the exaggerations contained in the article in question. The interview would not have attracted our attention had we not been struck, in the lines so generously published by *Familia,* by assertions that raise doubts about our cultural policy and do so in a manner worthy of a better cause. Aspersions are cast on writers of pro-Party patriotic poetry and prose. *Săptămîna* wishes to reiterate its solemn commitment to promoting literature of a deeply pro-Party, patriotic nature, and opposes such regrettable attitudes as mentioned, which deliberately ignore our present literary values and our desire to give voice to the policies of our Communist party in a spirit and form favorable to artistic creativity.

The "writers of pro-Party patriotic poetry and prose" and the Institution were upset that I had raised the "matter" of "the article in question," namely "Ideals." Under international pressure, *Săptămîna* had acknowledged the anti-Semitic "exaggerations" in such hackneyed phrases that the exaggerations were confirmed rather than repudiated.

The hit squad immediately joined in the attack. In the January 22 issue of *Flacăra,* Anonymous attacked my "liberaloid gesticulations"; he said that I had underrated "those with whom I shared my profession, but seemingly not my beliefs." On February 5, the same Anonymous implied that I did not know Romanian, and that I had "foreign" habits and manners. Meanwhile, the Lyric Pump wrote in the January 29 issue, "Even if you were to share a table in a tavern with this Norman Manea—with whom and whose work I am not acquainted, and yet who, I understand, has insulted me in an interview—you can still sit in the literary pantheon with Shakespeare." The sentence puzzled me. At a stretch, the reference to Shakespeare was understandable, given Păunescu's aspirations. The reference to the tavern, however, I did not understand. Several years later I learned that he had read at least one of my novels, and had been annoyed by a scene set in a tavern in which it seems he recognized himself. Comprehensible or not, Păunescu's "remarks" had no other purpose than to avoid responding to the question raised in my interview by simply shouting me down. (The fact that at the end of his piece Păunescu wrote my name without any capital letters conforms to a special grammar that reached its height in 1990 when, after the tyrant had been slain by his own nomenklatura, the "courageous" began to write his name in lowercase.)

For months at a time, *Săptămîna, Flacăra,* or *Luceafărul* would call me now Stalinist, now liberaloid; they accused me of "Archangelist descent," of being perfectly "synchronic" with Radio Free Europe, charged that I dreamed of becoming "prosecutor extraordinary of Romanian letters," and even that I addressed myself only to "those who live across the English Channel." This was a state of siege not unlike what other writers and artists on the Institution's blacklist had also endured.

"Have any other writers tried to protect you, or respond to the backbiting?" disinformation agent Cat asked with a sly smile, adjusting the crease of his elegant pants.

During these nightmarish months I did have the support and affection of my friends, as I did before and afterward. But public support? There was none. But I was not the only one to be denounced by the hit squad (although the attacks took on a special nationalistic color in my case) and any efforts to express support publicly would have met with insurmountable barriers. One fellow writer called me from the provinces to ask jokingly, but with perceptible anxiety, "Have they broken your windows yet?" Another, also in the provinces, urged me to write to him about the interview as a way of letting off steam. I remember with special warmth a distinguished author of the older generation who in a debate at the Writers' Association in Bucharest praised my book *October, Eight O'Clock,* which had come out at the same time as the interview and was also attacked. (In the spring of 1990 I had the pleasure of meeting him again in Paris: he was Romania's ambassador to France for a few months before the new nomenklatura, frightened by his independence, recalled him. I gave him the French translation of the book, which had just come out, some ten years after the original.)

And yet I was protected. . . .

I was protected indirectly, through the reviews of *October, Eight O'Clock* published in the fall of 1981, a few months after the interview. (It had not been easy to get them published: the author's name created a special tension. The first review came out only in February 1982, in *România Literară,* Romania's leading literary journal. I learned later that the day before that issue was to come out, the author of the review and several of his colleagues stayed in the editorial office to make sure that the piece was not withdrawn at the last minute, perhaps even after the type had been set.) Several important literary critics praised the book. They ridiculed the attacks on the interview and on me. They related their comments to my earlier books as well, placing these in the greater context of contemporary Romanian literature. Thus the argument had shifted from the ethical to the aesthetic and to the relationship between the two, a subject hard to avoid in a totalitarian regime.

Săptămîna reacted swiftly. The young rhymester Corneliu violently criticized *October, Eight O'Clock,* declaring that it was without literary value, that in it "nausea floats everywhere," "free love is practiced," that it "concentrates so much wretchedness and disgust" that the revolted reader, overwhelmed by a "gagging sensation," is obliged to protest, "Who needs a book like this? What kind of education are we giving the younger generation, who will judge us harshly if we renounce the healthy principles of Romanian culture . . . ?"

At the same time there was an unexpected desertion from the ranks of my disparagers. The Lyric Pump no longer poured out a gross stream of filth, but began pumping in a different direction. This was unexpected but not wholly surprising. The Pump was more talented, cleverer, and more manipulative than the others. Was he being sincere, or was it a calculated step in view of the rivalry between him and the younger poet for the good graces of the Ruling Family? The sudden rift in the group was of course a boon to me. But the manner in which I was "protected" proved as bizarre as the attack. The title of his article, "Valued by Being Added," seemed to imply that it might in the end be necessary to grant me my rights as a literary citizen, that is, as a "foreigner" favored with acceptance and naturalized, so to speak, by "being added."

Yet the poet's sudden revolt was only a passing, tactical disagreement within the group:

> I feel the need to stand up in opposition to the actions of the journal run by Eugen Barbu, smearing the literary and moral reputation of Norman Manea, a writer who must and does exist; the author of this criticism, Corneliu Vadim Tudor, who has in fact been responsible for many gaffes (some of them with serious consequences for the cultural world in general and for Eugen Barbu in particular), is hitting below the belt.

One of Corneliu's indiscriminate "gaffes" was no doubt the publication of "Ideals." It was significant that this piece should be called a gaffe, not an infamy. Nor were the precautions the Lyric Pump took to cover himself with respect to the Boss and the hit squad without significance:

> Of course I do not equate the merits of Barbu and Manea, but neither can I deny that Norman Manea will rightly be considered an important writer, if he is not already.

It was a useless precaution, however, as far as the Lyric Pump's comrades in the pro-Party patriotic program were concerned. The group promptly "unmasked" the traitor in one of its newspapers by doing just what the Lyric Pump had avoided: "Eugen Barbu is put on the very same level as Norman Manea, who was unknown as a writer until he created a furor in *Familia.*"

But it was the Pump's rival Corneliu who struck the coup de

grâce. In a long article entitled "Value by Discernment," he criticized not only the lack of aesthetic value and the dangerous political positions of *October, Eight O'Clock,* but also the poetry of the unassailable Pump. This time Corneliu seemed more tolerant of the artistic deficiencies of my books, but he could not conceal the "ideological deficiencies of the work," the fact that it makes fun of "the leading ideas of Party documents and policy," that "the early period of the building of socialism in Romania, together with some of the enduring ideas of Marxism," are distorted and ridiculed, and that it challenges "the Party's just policy on religion, which is entirely free in Romania, both in theory and in practice."

However, Corneliu left out the crowning accusation, which was probably reserved for my file: the fact that in my short story "Robot Biography" there is a shady Party apparatchik, whose birthday is on January 26, who proposes that "Luck" (that is, lottery winnings) should be secretly directed by the Party toward "worthy workers." Not even officer Corneliu dared reveal in print this incredible insolence to the Most Beloved Son of the People, whose birthday occasioned, every January 26, grotesque displays of general hypocrisy and flattery, including the obligatory participation of the whole nationwide circus.

Corneliu limited himself to one persuasive example. He quoted the words "Let's fool the phantom of Boredom that is haunting the world." He correctly pointed out that this is "a paraphrase of the opening words of the *Communist Manifesto:* 'A specter is haunting Europe.' In Marx's classic work it is 'the specter of communism,' while for N.M. communism has metamorphosed into boredom."

A solemn, sullen dictatorship. Beneath the apparent solidity it was without substance. The Authority's rhetoric took advantage of serious principles by continually perverting them.

How could one "resist" in this world of the absurd? Isn't every attempt to be authentic, to rehabilitate the truth, inevitably prey to manipulation and defacement?

Anyone who did not want to give in to the Terror's lies and travesties suffered not only fear but often a deep sense of uselessness. I had avoided solemnity in my conversation with the Securitate officer, but my doubts, before and after my dialogue with him, were just as great as my fear before and after the interview was published. But I knew that too much "seriousness" would look ridiculous in the world of the ridiculous. I hoped that the sense of uselessness that often overwhelmed me was something entirely different from vacuousness; I tried to express my melancholy in irony and my fears in sarcasm.

How ridiculous does the poor stubborn truth-teller look in a world where everything is ridiculous, in a setting that is fractured, disfigured, and dominated by mummers and masquerades? Does confronting the absurd put an end to absurdity? The nasty little devil who was constantly and everywhere occupied with his nasty, dirty business was still an active threat: when he did not kill his enemy he poisoned everything around him, he smothered everybody in the stinking farce that was undermining the society. What could be salvaged from a totalitarian world of filth, and how? The integrity of anyone who struggled to salvage life was threatened not only by the Tyrant's prisons and security forces, but equally by the secret, diabolical mechanisms of distortion, perversion, and caricature ceaselessly at work. The Tyrant's mask was watching everywhere. From all the walls in the whole totalitarian circus, portraits of the great clown smirked victoriously over Auguste the Fool, who alone refused to fall into line.

The door closed. I waited for the sound of the elevator. The officer must have walked down. I waited. What if he came back? What if his button came off again? That socialist thread was no good, I knew; it might not be strong enough for his triumphal descent of the stairs. What if he suddenly told me something completely unexpected, what if he had forgotten to make the real point? Just when the prey had relaxed, sure that he had passed the test, that's when an unexpected blow could be fatal. But he did not come back.

It was a beautiful day in June. I walked around the city for a few hours. Had I perhaps tried to see more than was there, in that silly meeting? I had not forgotten the months when I bought the papers daily just to see what new attack lay in store. Had I exaggerated those outpourings of hatred and filth?

I did not want to accept the ethnic corner in which the Authority was trying to isolate me. The child who had come back from the concentration camp at the end of the war wanted at all cost to forget, at all cost to be like everyone else. Forty years later, must I again feel a victim? I could not bear it. I mistrusted those who professionalized their laments and I hated those who provoked them.

"There are times when we must sink to the bottom of our misery to understand truth," Václav Havel writes in *The Power of the Powerless*. I had had many occasions to touch "the bottom of our misery," in childhood, adolescence, and adulthood; as one of the "elect" in our insatiable century, I did not need to go through it again to clarify my thinking. But the man from the Securitate had polarized both old and new questions. Perhaps in a concentration camp (and what was Romania during Ceauşescu's last decade but a concentration camp the size of a collapsing country?) it is indecent for prisoners with glasses to complain of their extra humiliations, when the situation is desperate for all. And yet . . . There is the danger that a guard could knock someone's glasses to the ground, then chase the myopic captive around. He would stumble, confused, while the brutal mob would laugh, and this cannot be ignored. The excessive suffering of the individual (and what can suffering be except individual, even in the setting of a collective tragedy?) cannot be denied, even in the face of great general suffering. Is there something, then, beyond what is recognized as unbearable? Yes, when an individual perceives an "excess" as yet more unbearable than the unbearable. Was I justified in thinking that I had reached that level?

The smear campaign in the press in 1982, and the protocol visit from the Securitate man in 1985, and all else that happened at the time and earlier, served to remind me again and again that I was living under a perverse system, and any resistance also bore the mark of the "model of the captive world," a world in which all sides are somehow tainted. Under these circumstances, was not Havel's "living within the truth," as I had tried to do, as vain as isolating myself in Havel's "hidden spheres" in which I had tried to defend my identity and from which I had suddenly emerged into the ring?

In order to understand what happened in the course of half a century in Eastern Europe, one must understand how difficult it was to state a normal, obvious, ordinary thought in public, and the fact that there were only brief periods when this could be risked. But even when it was not as dangerous as during Stalinist times, a banal truth could never be spoken simply and directly—in contrast to the official lies that sprawled shamelessly in full view. For this reason the banal lie in its grossness will be easier for a future reader to decode. Now the bomb's powder has been dampened, prohibitions have been removed, and the code has been almost forgotten. In fact a number of writers are feeling an undeniable gloom over this, because what only a few years ago was explosive and written at terrible risk has suddenly lost its impact.

The banalities I was so proud of publishing readily struck the eye. Apparently they struck the censors too and made them popeyed with fury. Still, it may be hard for the uninitiated to understand the "explosive" lines in my interview.

Was the banal claim that during the postwar period "humanity was shaken by the testimony and the appeal of great literary consciences" a reference to Solzhenitsyn and others like him? Was the banal statement that in order for a "public person to be the authentic emanation of universal aspirations, there is a need, first of all, for real public opinion" a reference to the Great Conducător? The dictator was, according to the press, the "representative" of the people's "universal aspirations"—even if under his enlightened dictatorship (the Ceauşescu years were called "years of enlightenment" by writers of "pro-Party patriotic poetry and prose") the condition of the country continually worsened. What about clichés like "open confrontation of opinions" or "exact and wide-ranging information" or "protection of privacy and of choice"? Were these ironic references to the *only* Party and to an *expanded* Securitate? To regulations against contact with foreigners and against abortion, to gynecological examinations at work, and to the presence in every workplace of a Securitate officer?

What about the banal assertion that "there is now a pompous, deliberately celebratory aspect in newspaper pages that at times takes on incredible proportions"? Even a child could guess in whose honor those celebratory pages were produced. The fact that this banality was printed by a Romanian publication of this period is explained by the obvious observation that in contrast to the Stalinist period, "the price of conformism and the price of courage are much diminished today, while the guilt of those who commit themselves to twisting the truth and abusing language becomes obviously greater. . . ."

There is another kind of code as well. Even the comment that so shook the text specialists of the circus's Central Committee can be understood only by the initiate: ". . . a still-young rhymester, recycled by a Herder fellowship, served up a warmed-over editorial, dreadful and chauvinistic, entitled—what else?—'Idealuri' ('Ideals'), the likes of which I did not believe we would ever again read in Romania. We need not go into its regrettable consequences here; suffice it to say that the young man, very eager to resuscitate a nostalgia for other times, was not fired and demoted, for the purpose of rest and therapy, to, let us say, a journal like *Albina* (*The Bee*) or *Sănătatea* (*Health*), but he is before television cameras and among the leading echelons of the press." The young rhymester was Corneliu, of course, the one who wanted to replace the Lyric Pump in the eyes of the Great Incendiary. It should be mentioned too that the Herder grant did not come from any Herr Herder but from Comrade the Boss of the "cultural journal that has acquired an unfortunate reputation," that is, *Săptămîna*. "Nostalgia for other times" was a reference to the Fascist slogans of the Romanian right during the period between the wars; the chauvinist editorial "Ideals" eagerly gave these new life, and did so with official encouragement.

Nor could the reader understand even this line without knowing the code: ". . . a writer angered by the critics churned out, for months on end, a vehement, black series of articles against the most important of them. This writer published these articles in book form, not in Romania but in Italy. . . ." The reader would have to know about the assistance given the hit squad by Iosif Constantin Drăgan, a Romanian émigré living in Italy who had, after the war, acquired considerable wealth: a collaborator of Ceaușescu and a supporter of the Romanian "new right," an echo of the far right of which he had been a member between the wars.

My interview infuriated the censors precisely because they knew the code. But didn't its very existence weaken the message? Perhaps not, at least at that time, since the officials had made the interview a "state problem." I also made an ironic comment about the "prefabricated panel of eminent figures," that is, the official writers. But I went on to defend books on political subjects, books the Boss affirmed had been published "with permission from the police." Rereading those lines I smiled. In reality still more footnotes are required. I would have had to explain that the new generation of the nomenklatura had begun to write "literature." That according to the Byzantine traditions of the land they were allowed critical "insolences" others could not dream of. That their writing was indeed done with police permission, but that the Boss—who else?—actually wanted to throw suspicion on any writer who made the slightest effort to uncover any real truth about the national masquerade.

Explanations, codes, details, blown up to grotesque proportions. "There nothing goes and everything matters—here everything goes and nothing matters," Philip Roth wrote, comparing Eastern Europe and the West. Yes, the story of the interview was much longer than the interview; the story of each sentence could be as long as the entire text.

The truth survived in fractured, codified form and only because of the stubborn determination of those who still believed in it. "Why do you go on preaching when you know you can't change the lost souls?" a rabbi was asked. "So as not to change myself," he answered. The code was more important than the text, backstage more important than the performance. Life went on underground for most.

The public uproar over my interview in *Familia* aggravated my far from idyllic relation with the power.

The wolves increased in size and number, and more lights were trained on me. No further references to the interview were permitted in the press. The piece was pulled from *The Anthology of the Romanian Interview*, although those who put the anthology together had tried to include it. It was also dropped from my 1984 *On the Fringes,* a book of essays rejected by the censors (who claimed that it was entirely "in the spirit" of the interview) but later published at the courageous insistence of a worthy editor and friend.

The officer, who had been sent to demonstrate that the Institution could dissociate itself, when it wanted, from some of its servants (like the hit squad) and that it valued the "European type," clearly knew all about what had happened around the interview. It is safe to assume that he was on to the recent panic in the Writers' Union when a jury almost awarded me a prize for *October, Eight O'Clock* (that jury would later imprudently award me a prize for *On the Fringes,* but the officials who valued my "European type" withdrew it). The officer who had touchingly remarked that I "looked like his father" certainly was aware, when he asked why I did not emigrate, that there would be hard times ahead for me if I tried to publish another book.

And yet when I got my long-awaited passport in September 1985,

I left *The Black Envelope,* a book even more violently critical of the system than all the rest, with my publisher. I returned after two months abroad to hopeless Romania. The problems in getting my new book published in 1986 surpassed even my most pessimistic expectations. If it had not been for the support of my editor friends it would never have come out, not even after many cuts and changes. The situation in the country was growing ever more dangerous, and my own had probably reached its limits. In 1986, I applied again for permission to go to the West as a "tourist"—this time with my wife. After a long wait we both got passports.

There was no visit from the Securitate, though. I was braced for the warning telephone call (from "Minorities"? from "Literature"?). Before leaving I reread the reply I had made to the attacks on this "foreign" Romanian writer whose language was supposedly not Romanian. It was indirect, of course. My article had come out in the Jewish journal *Revista Cultului Mozaic* on March 15, 1982. I had made use of the "ethnic" pigeonhole where I had been put; indeed, I probably could not have published it anywhere else. A review of a collection of Giorgio Bassani's short stories, it was also entitled, significantly, "Within Walls":

> Bassani is as Italian as Bellow is American and Modiano French (and with difficulty we refrain from mentioning here the names of some remarkable contemporary Romanian prose writers whose unfortunate linguistic isolation—and not only linguistic—precludes them from receiving the international renown they deserve . . .). Giorgio Bassani is a "universal" writer as all important writers are, whether their names be Saba, Schultz, Blecher, Canetti, or Chekhov, or Mann, or many others of today or yesterday. They belong to their own place and time and origins, and at the same time to everyone everywhere and always.

The journal that ran this piece had a very limited circulation. And yet the response came quickly—in *Săptămîna* once again, under the byline of the less and less young rhymester Corneliu.

Mentioning the piece "that appeared in the latest issues of a Bucharest journal" (which he modestly refrained from naming), he wrote, "the list of names, ostensibly random, has a hidden meaning that we understand; we do not, however, understand what a *Blecher* or a *Schultz* is doing among 'universal' writers like Chekhov and Thomas Mann." Useless to explain to someone who ignored Saba and Canetti just who are Blecher (considered by the French a kind of Romanian Kafka) or Bruno Schultz (his Polish counterpart). Referring to other "comments that raise doubts about Norman Manea's 'ideology,' " the Institution asked rhetorically, "What does 'and not only linguistic' isolation mean?" and concluded, "We would like to know whom he has in mind, and in what sense are they isolated so that they cannot become world writers?! As for linguistic isolation, we might inform N.M. that he can never himself aspire to universality in a foreign language, since he does not even know Romanian." Clearly Corneliu was not only going against the opinions of literary critics regarding my work; more fundamentally, he was questioning whether I, as a "foreigner," belonged to the language and to the country. Even if this were just a nationalist tune (or perhaps precisely because it was?), it was a painful barb. Many writers before me, in all literatures, have said that "the writer's language is his country." A poet added, "even when the language is German and the writer is Jewish." That was the exiled Paul Celan.

It was perhaps not surprising that in the very next issue of *Săptămîna* an article called "Necessary Ideology" specified more precisely how Corneliu envisioned "the creation of a new man." To this creation "artists and cultural figures were called to give of their best." The nonconforming elements in society were to fall by the wayside, beginning with those who (even if they wrote in Romanian) were not ethnically and culturally Romanian. "Like it or not, there will be a natural selection. Because morally you cannot live off the work of a people and defy them with your imagined superiority, or be paid by such a humane Communist regime when you are its number one faultfinder, or write in Romanian when at the same time you make fun of the anonymous authors of *Miorița* and *Master Manole,* and of Eminescu, Iorga, Goga, and others." He was referring to masterpieces of Romanian folklore and to Romanian classics of nationalist bent. No one had made fun of the sacred "traditional values," as was claimed. This was just an imputation of guilt that was to lead to "natural selection"—an insinuation that those who might commit sacrilege, who were by virtue of their birth destined to commit it, had in fact committed it.

When the Minorities officer asked me about emigrating, was this connected to this false praise of the "European type"? Was it possible that in 1985 the Securitate had read words that were still in Danilo Kiš's head, that were not even written in Romanian? I refer to a piece Danilo Kiš published in 1987, about a writer from Eastern Europe who gradually discovers that the source of his conflict with the authorities and its consequences (marginalization and oppression) make up his latent "European consciousness," since "consciousness of belonging to Central Europe is itself in the end a kind of dissidence." I came across the Danilo Kiš piece outside Romania. "Like the Jew who wants to prove that he is assimilated, this writer then discovers that the misunderstanding arises from his own reserve, from his almost unconscious aspiration toward a European horizon that is more democratic and more comprehensive—the very thing he is accused of. The result of his awakening is exile. Or prison." I recognized myself in this description, more than in any other. The awakening came slowly; the conflict was insoluble; the separation painful.

The relationship between my past and my present fits into a broader context than the events I am describing here. I left Romania in 1986, and the distance in time from the last decade has become a distance in space as well. Not that I was ever a lover of travel. I was expelled from Romania for the first time at age five, for the last at age fifty. These were the consequences of a tumultuous history in which the significant experiences of the century—the Holocaust, totalitarianism, exile—were reserved for the "chosen."

In 1990 I came across, in a German magazine *(Weimarer Beiträge)*, a description of my situation at the time I left. Its conclusions can be summed up in a few lines: "The moment he picked was almost too late. Manea could not be corrupted and he could not be ignored. When he finally decided with heavy heart to leave, he had reason to expect a worse fate at any moment: to disappear without a trace into the Securitate dungeons." The article, "Das 'Perpetuum Mobile' des Verstossung" ("The 'Perpetuum Mobile' of Repudiation"), was written by Eva Behring, a well-known scholar of Romanian literature and someone very familiar with postwar Romania.

The danger of disappearing into the Securitate dungeons was hypothetical. I had occasion to address it in the United States in 1988. A professor considering my application for a grant asked what would happen to me if I returned to Romania. Would I be jailed? Would I be killed? A rather brutal question, true, but justified by his desire to have that grant used efficiently. The committee had already been startled when I said that I was not a "dissident" as that term is now understood. I had not been a member of the Communist party, and no book or shorter piece of mine contained any shameful kowtowing to the system. I had extremely rarely used the word "comrade," and only then in an ironic sense. But neither had I become a fanatical anti-Communist, as might have been expected. I had tried to live "within the truth" as a writer, in a time and place and political system where normality was suspect. My conflict with the authorities "has not come about through any conscious intention" but simply "through the inner logic" of my "thinking, behavior, or work," to quote Havel on dissidents. But it would be going too far to give myself a label that has acquired, perhaps rightly, a much narrower definition. As an "outsider" I had found my condition best described in Danilo Kiš's concept of the European.

My answer to the committee was: I don't know. Maybe I would be arrested if I returned to Romania, or maybe just interrogated, or maybe nothing would happen to me, maybe I would be "accidentally" run over, maybe I would commit suicide. Anything could happen, or nothing. The truth was, I didn't know. Given the hateful, duplicitous nature of the system, no sure prediction could be made, although friends from Romania whom I met in Berlin in 1987 warned me not to return under any circumstances.

The paradoxical nature of Romanian communism in the last decade defied logic in a completely different way from the previous Stalinist period, although there were some similarities. Ceauşescu's dictatorship was of a Stalinist and Nazi type, granted, but its "new" features (borrowed from dictatorships of both left and right, from Latin America, Asia, and Africa) were superimposed in a bizarre fashion on basically Byzantine roots. The pervasive double-dealing might strike at any moment from unexpected quarters. The ambiguous relationship between the overseers and the overseen often had paradoxically surprising positive effects. Setting aside some important national differences, these characteristics are essential to an understanding of the "real socialism" found throughout all the countries of Eastern Europe in the last decades.

The publication of the interview, that of *October, Eight O'Clock,* and of the work of other "rebellious slaves" are good examples. Without the "support" of the system's ambiguity, it would have been impossible to find, even if intermittently, the kind of solidarity, honesty, or resistance necessary to be published and reviewed. This is not of course to minimize the hysterical defensive reaction displayed by officialdom when it sensed danger. What the system perceived as a threat became one, especially in the area of ideas and of language. Even during relatively elastic periods when the government seemed to understand that a breath of air would not necessarily lead to the collapse of the system but rather to a brief adjustment of society's metabolism (in 1981 the situation in Romania was already incomparably worse than during the period of pretended "liberalization," but infinitely better than what followed), still, when the rules of the game were broken, the official reaction and the rush to reestablish appearances revealed the same brutish and ridiculous panic.

Under these circumstances, how do you avoid a terrible sense of pointlessness in the face of grotesque battles—now blown up, now reduced to nothing, now seen as in a distorting mirror and now as in a nightmare? "In the enormous silence produced by official repression and fear, one can hear a pin drop," Mary McCarthy said. How can you know whether the blow that shook the circus's tent was not the sound of a pin dropping?

A non-Romanian reader in 1982 or 1992 would probably have trouble understanding what was so subversive about my interview. Probably Romanian readers too will very soon find it difficult. The system was steadily weakened by slow corrosion until it collapsed by a lucky conjunction of circumstances. It is also true that the agony could have gone on for a longer time, for the system produced a stupor that tended to protect it. Was the irony (and often the sarcasm) that the system provoked just, as was asked in the famous interview, "an epiphany of the derisory"?

Is anything revealed by the overlong story of that interview (interesting and tedious as life in the realm of the absurd)? Is banality, in truth or in lie, ever revealing? What about the details through which God and the devil reveal their ironic game? For instance, the details of the way that piece came out. Even if it was but "a pin dropping," the interview echoed like a bomb blast at official levels. The basic question (why was its publication allowed?) was extremely serious, at least in its consequences. But the answer is a funny one, at least potentially, as befits an "epiphany of the derisory." The dictator was trying out a new move, crooked and risky, to strengthen censorship by "turning it over to the working people." The piece was published because somebody from the "working people" liked making trips to Korea: that somebody was the editor-in-chief of the journal that printed it. Editors-in-chief were appointed by the Party and were personally responsible for everything in their publications. Only when they were away could

somebody else make a decision. In this case, someone else seized the
moment and took the risk. Indeed *Săptămîna* would claim in one
of its denunciations that it was only because the person (politically)
responsible "was in Korea or China for half a year" that *Familia*
"published what it published." But on his return from the land of
"peaceful mornings," as our sister dictatorship of North Korea was
called, the politically responsible-in-chief of *Familia* published
these self-critical words:

> The fact that the things you speak of were done while I was out
> of the country does not in any way mitigate their distressing effects.
> Our journal has published a great many well-guided articles on
> literary theory and criticism, but unfortunately it has also shown, as
> you note, a drift toward cosmopolitanism, involuntarily striking at
> the national spirit of our literature and even maligning that spirit.

I would only discover in 1990, almost ten years later, what really lay
behind this declaration.

The dictator was killed in December 1989. Since then Romania has
been undergoing a confused and difficult transition. A large part of
the old administration has been retained ("The sons of our rulers
will rule our children" is a current saying); the economy is a
shambles; the old Securitate is still active in the shadows (under the
name Romanian Information Service, the SRI) and dispersed
through many other branches of the state machinery; in addition to
this, much of the population is oppressed by feelings of guilt, fear,
and vengeance, the heritage of the dictatorship's pathological opportunism and the universal hatred it inspired. Many things remain
unchanged, but some changes can be seen. At least it is to be hoped
that the "direction" has changed, as a wise commentator has said.
Until December 1989, Romania was going against the current,
moving toward a more closed and oppressive society, and now let's
hope it is going with the current, moving toward democracy, in

spite of frequent breakdowns, detours, and even backtracking.

There has been a highly visible change in the press. About one thousand new journals have appeared, of all types, orientations, and levels of quality. Some are excellent, good enough to compete with any publication in the world; others are worse than the most wretched papers anywhere. There is room for more honesty and intelligence and originality in the press now. There is also, paradoxical as it may seem, room for even more filth, lying, and perversion than there was under that capacious dictatorship.

The civic duty is fulfilled by a part of the free press that discusses the effects of right- or left-wing totalitarianism, uncovers the mechanisms of complicity and displays of self-abasement, and develops a curriculum for democracy. But the rehabilitation of the Securitate and of the nomenklatura, the return of xenophobia and anti-Westernism, disinformation, the manipulation of confusion and resentment, seem to be the immediate objectives of another segment of the press, which is putting its new "freedom" to use by continuing its wicked game.

Several figures connected in one way or another with the 1981 interview are examples of this significant trend. As at the beginning of the decade, when the dictatorship was evolving into its grimmest stage, now, when the first paths to democracy are being worked out, my "case" may help one understand the general situation. Again, it is only in the context of history, even up to the present, that the long story of the interview reveals its meaning and justifies the telling.

As I already said, it was only in the spring of 1990 that I learned, from an article in a Bucharest journal, what repercussions were suffered by those who had pushed through the publication of the interview. Radu Enescu has only now said what, out of consideration for the subject of the interview, he did not say then. Enescu was not only publicly repudiated by his chief; he was also dismissed:

> Taking advantage of the absence from the country of my "decisive factor," I published an interview with Norman Manea in which he

protested for the first time against the chauvinistic nationalism and anti-Semitism espoused by a weekly in the capital which had direct links to the Dynamo Club—sorry, the Tricolor Union. I need not remind you of what followed then in the Council of Culture, where the interview became a state problem, in the office of today's columnist of *Democraţia,* etc.

This may be a useful key to a rereading of that interview, and also to the present situation. No need to explain what kind of thing would become a *state problem* in the world of the derisory; no surprise that the consequences would be far from absurd. The first public protest against official nationalism was taken as a real anti-government act by the Securitate (which Radu Enescu ironically calls the Dynamo Club, the former name of the Securitate sports club, which in 1990 changed its name to the Tricolor Union). Nothing unexpected about defaming the person who protested: that was the most appropriate form of punishment in the world of the absurd, because insinuation, insult, and filth are ultraefficient in a world without substance and of tragic farce. But there is obviously a connection to the present as well. The former secretary of the Central Committee in charge of ideology, who in 1981 was hysterical when the interview appeared, became in 1990 a columnist for the journal *Democraţia.* After the collapse of the dictatorship (but not of its supporters), two of the best-known practitioners of the profession of self-abasement, Anonymous and this former Party activist, started a new paper under the "liberalized" press laws, choosing, of course, a suitable name, *Democraţia.* This is not the only odd change in post-Ceauşescu Romania. *Săptămîna,* which has been discussed so much in this account, is still run by the Boss and Corneliu under a new name, *România Mare (Great Romania).* This journal has also set up a foundation by the same name, and even a Committee for the Investigation of Anti-Romanian Activities. Previously financed by the Party, the journal suffers from no shortage of funds today. Like countless others who took part in and were favored by the dictatorship, the Boss is not a poor man. The public, always looking for entertainment, ensures a wide readership for the insults and diversions he prints. It's possible the editors were telling the truth when they claimed not to need financial assistance from abroad. In any event, tactically it would not have been wise to admit that support came from the same source now as before, namely from the far-right-wing Romanian in Italy, Iosif Constantin Drăgan (who, incidentally, was declared a "Fascist, a Legionary, and a collaborator in the Ceauşescu regime" on November 30, 1990, by a tribunal in Milan, in a case brought by the Italian journal *Panorama*). Mr. Drăgan, the former Fascist and supporter of *Săptămîna,* is now an honored guest of Ion Iliescu, the current president, and his Romanian tentacles are spread not only to *România Mare* but also to many other channels in the Romanian press and mass media.

România Mare no longer belongs to the Party Municipality of Bucharest but calls itself an "absolutely independent weekly." The motto on the banner is no longer "Workers of the World Unite," but an equally stirring "We Will Be Again What We Were, And More." *România Mare*'s program is even better suited to the new slogan than the old. The rehabilitation of the Securitate, the maligning of dissidents, an instigation to nationalism, a yearning for the days of the dictatorship, and anti-Western campaigns are the major concerns of this publication. The conversion from *Săptămîna* to *România Mare* was made without ideological difficulties. In December 1989, shortly before Ceauşescu was killed, *Săptămîna* toed the line, maintaining that the demonstration in Timişoara that sparked the changes in Romania had been organized by troublemakers instigated by foreign powers (especially Hungary). Soon after the dictator's death this line was taken up by *România Mare.*

There are oddities about the journal as well. It holds that Romania was repeatedly betrayed by the West ("a country coveted by all, at the center of an endless international plot"), that it was sold at Yalta, and that in 1989 its "great patriot" was disposed of in Malta by the two superpowers in a secret agreement. That "great patriot" is of course none other than . . . the dictator himself. This is how they describe Ceauşescu (in 1990!): "One of the greatest men in our nation's history. It was certainly he who, as the natural representative of the Romanian people—quite apart from his dedication and his great industry and intelligence—gave our history *planetary dimensions and consequence*" (emphasis theirs). They praise the Romanian people for "being ready, in spite of considerable sacrifice, to erect for their leader a palace four times as large as the Louvre of the French kings." Reference is made to the palace ordered by Romania's Ubu Roi during his last decades; it was to be a show of "gratitude" from the country he had terrorized and starved. But to the editors of *România Mare,* the disastrous situation Ceaușescu brought about and maintained is of different origin: "The West starved us for ten years." And there are other startling assertions, equally original: "There was one good thing about Ceaușescu: he presented us with the country, so to speak, free of foreign debt," or "he did leave us something, whether it be revitalized cities, the subway, or education for all." Securitate officers are considered "true patriots"; former dissidents and intellectuals opposing the present regime are represented as coming "from the Zionist and right-wing movements" ("the monstrous coalition"), or from "that Galician-Phanariot yeast" formed of "people who are always scheming, planning diversions; if you look carefully into their backgrounds you will be surprised to find that they are of Fascist origins, or that they have relatives in Jerusalem: They are the ones who are strangling this country." Hungarians are represented as a "bloodthirsty people who have caused bloodbaths at the crossroads of history." The tireless Corneliu took it upon himself to write an interminable anti-Hungarian series entitled "Watch Out for Hungary"; in these articles he suggested not only that Ceaușescu's overthrow had been planned by the Soviets and the Americans and carried out by Hungarians (and that the Securitate with its patriotic martyrs was the only organization that tried to resist this diabolical plan), but also that, in order to annex Transylvania, Hungary is preparing to go to war with Romania.

However, since Romania is no longer the exclusive property of the dictator and his family, the hit squad that *România Mare* brought back to life (with the help of the "transformed" Institution) can produce only a limited degree of oppression. Under the new circumstances, *România Mare* has been answered more than once by democratic publications and by people who can no longer be stopped by censors.

Now it is even possible to take public action to unmask the activities of the hit squad. For instance, in the fall of 1990 the Writers' Union decided to exclude the Boss from its ranks. The reason for this decision offers a useful guide to anyone wishing to understand the Ceauşescu years and the present period of transition:

> During the last decades, Eugen Barbu transformed *Săptămîna*, of which he was editor-in-chief, into an undisguised organ of the Ceauşescu Securitate service, slandering the works and the characters of Romania's outstanding writers and cultural figures. Eugen Barbu is guilty of skillful literary plagiarism, a crime that was made public in 1979 at a meeting of the Leadership Council of the Writers' Union. Nicolae Ceauşescu himself prevented this plagiarist's file from being made public. At present, Eugen Barbu is editor-in-chief of *România Mare,* essentially a Fascist journal, in which even more scandalously he persists in the style and mode of thought that were seen in *Săptămîna* and in so doing contributes to the deterioration of the moral and political climate of the country.

And here, at the start of a new era, the Lyric Pump raised his voice in public once again, this time to *defend* Eugen Barbu. The life of the official troubadour has been stormy since the death of his patron. After his miraculous escape in December 1989, he retreated into meditation and calculation, only to reappear, immaculate and revived, determined to be once again what he had been and more. Never short of money, he established his own publishing house (ah, the advantages of democracy!) and has published an immense volume of his own poetry intended to show that under the dictatorship his right hand had been writing one thing while his left another. He is the editor of widely distributed journals and even has one of his own, *Şi totuşi iubirea* (*And Yet Love*). And now the soulful poet vehemently protested the Boss's disgrace: the Boss, with whom he has always had an uneasy love-hate relationship, now embracing him, now spitting on him, now managing to do both at once.

The present still belongs to the recent past, though visible efforts to disentangle one from the other are being made. The relationship between past and present cannot be expected to recover too quickly. Thus it is ironic and significant to see characters connected to the affair of the interview reappearing on stage—which is all the more ironic and significant since this is not an account of a heroic or an extraordinary occurrence. It is a run-of-the-mill story concerning an event and some characters that ordinarily would constitute a puzzling parenthesis rather than be memorialized in the pages of history.

In all fairness, as the tale draws to its open ending, we should also wonder about the officer whose name and mission and whose profession prevent him from showing himself in public: Where is he today and what name does he go by? Is he working at the Tricolor Union Club? Was he transferred to some new section, Democracy or Free Market? Or is he still working at the "Minorities and Diversions Section," an important job at all times? These are hardly unreasonable questions, since the shadows of Securitate are ubiquitous throughout the country. I wonder what he thought of the two short pieces that came out in the fall of 1990, tied in a rather obscure but profound way to the interview he had referred to during our little performance of 1985.

On September 7, 1990, *România Mare* publicly celebrated "the tenth anniversary of the publication of 'Ideals' in *Săptămîna.*" In 1980, the piece was published unsigned; now the journal revealed the name of its author, Corneliu, a name many people already knew. This was done so that the author, freed by "democracy," could finally express his opinions and even be shown as a surviving martyr holding steadfast to his own beliefs. The commemorative article explains that "a tremendous uproar began at the time in the leading political forums and also abroad," and that "anti-Semitism was also stirred up by these enemies of Romania, who will do anything to invent Fascists where none exist."

The travesty and manipulation continues even today. Should we try to see humor in the claim of the persecutor that he was also a victim of persecution by the "leading political forums," the "people abroad," or by the "enemies of Romania"? I probably need only to reread a fragment of "Ideals":

> . . . the highest honors must be accorded to those who *perform patriotic deeds,* as the ancient chronicler said, and not to money-hungry visitors, to teachers of the democratic tarantella in their smelly old alpacas, to racketeers whose interests are foreign to those of this nation, who jingle their arrogance in their pockets and fool some people with their fake patriotism. We need no lazy prophets, no Judases in whose cheap and venal blood the heritage of Romanian sacrifice does not flow.

The irresistible magic of that text would justify, I hope even to Officer Cat, the length of the citation. It is not hard to imagine what he would say about it, given our discussion in 1985. Nor what he would say about an important announcement in the issue of *România Mare* that followed the one on the anniversary of "Ideals," declaring an annual celebration that would henceforth be held every September. The announcement explained why both the publication of "Ideals" and the celebration are set in this lovely autumn month, that "for the Romanians" there is a special significance to the date September 13, when "we honor everyone named Corneliu." It is not exactly the author of "Ideals" who is the patron saint of this day, but an illustrious predecessor: Corneliu Zelea-Codreanu, head of the Romanian Fascist movement between the wars, born on September 13, 1899.

Officer Cat would not of course be impressed by this noncoincidence. Nor would he probably be disturbed by a piece ("Mr. Ion Iliescu's Personal Securitate") published on November 30, 1990, by the retired Captain Adrian Ionescu, in which we learn that *"Ro-*

mânia Mare is for all practical purposes an organ of the Romanian Information Service." The fact that the Romanian Information Service is the new name of the former Securitate readily explains why the staff of *România Mare* enjoys, as Ionescu says, "free access to the service's building like any other employee of that institution."

On the occasion of the tenth anniversary of that interview and its ironic history, an instinctive mechanism brings to mind, in 1991, in the American woods where I now live, the words of a friend: "When you've been asked to pay more than others for the circus, you should feel really honored."

> Bard College
> January 1991
> *Translated by Alexandra Bley-Vroman*

NORMAN MANEA: ''THE WRITER —THAT CONSCIENCE IN WHICH HIS FELLOW MAN CAN BELIEVE.''*

GHEORGHE GRIGURCU: *Allow me, Norman Manea, if I may, to begin with a quote from Charles Dickens: "A man does not have the right to be a public person unless he makes himself the echo of public opinion." I would like to ask you, to what extent do you consider a writer to represent himself and to what extent is he a public person? Might there exist a conflict of interests here?*

NORMAN MANEA: A name inscribed in a book is perhaps man's supreme attempt at *solidarity* with his fellow man, in defiance of

---

* This interview, conducted in July 1981, appeared in the following form in *Familia*, December 1981, as part of the journal's "Conversing with the Epoch" series. It was translated by Cornelia Golna.

mortality. The world of literature represents at the same time the miraculous conversion of *solitary* suffering and hopes. This double and only apparently contradictory premise of an artist's work defines the rather unusual nature of this type of individual. "If he is profound, the artist inevitably offers a confession about himself, about the world in which he lives, and about the human condition," says Ernesto Sábato, a writer to whom I feel bound. Even if he does not manifest himself publicly except through his work, the true writer remains an ultrasensitive sensor, an acute warning signal. There are, nevertheless, times when even the most solitary men of letters are obliged to overcome their skepticism, to accept the risk of rhetoric. After all, even Émile Zola did it. . . . Even if we limit ourselves to the postwar period, we see that humanity was shaken by the testimony and the appeal of great literary consciences. It is wrong to believe, as some wish to convince us, that Romanian writers are merely "talented," "wavering," "frivolous," "Balkanic." Even the last Writers' Conference gave evidence of the convergence between literary values and civic conscience, in the form of an authentic and worthy spiritual commitment to the country's progress and culture.

In fact, Dickens's words could better serve as a guide for politicians. For a public person to be the authentic emanation of universal aspirations, there is a need, first of all, for real public opinion. This cannot, under any circumstance, result from the amorphous leveling and dehumanization of the individual, but must come from the polarization of individual values. In order for this to become possible, we would need exact and wide-ranging information, an open confrontation of opinions, the protection of privacy and of choice, the equal and free access of each individual to his own opinion—a publicly stated opinion, of course.

Any writer worthy of his serious mission would struggle to overcome this impasse, if it indeed exists, between solitude and solidarity.

G.G.: *Though I am aware of the unstable nature of the concept of myth (someone has concluded that it has been defined in any of five*

*hundred ways), I wish, nevertheless, to ask you if political life can
also be treated as a myth. What would be the arguments for and
against such a definition? Lucian Blaga[1] once told me that Lenin
practiced pure politics, just as others practice pure poetry. . . .*

N.M.: From the artistic point of view, some have achieved unusual,
spectacular effects in mythologizing political life. As far as I am
concerned, I prefer demythification, bringing everything back to the
real, terrestrial, human plane, scrutinizing this area of life with the
same fervor but also with the same lucidity as any other. I am not
an enthusiastic supporter of the tendency of some to create a
convergence of poetry and politics while ignoring the great differences between them. As far as purity is concerned . . . I worked for
many years in the field of water-quality control; water is a primor-
dial element (symbolic for some, but vital for all) of existence.
Water polluted to the point of degradation becomes an agent of
death, not life. On the other hand, artificially sterilized water does
not answer the normal, everyday needs of man either: the taste is
disgusting for the very fact that it lacks all taste, and its supply of
nutrients is wiped out. That is why we all, including reasonable,
clear-thinking politicians, prefer live, "humanized," potable water
as part of normal life.

G.G.: *In what way does the political factor enter into your personal
equation as a writer? Is it a stimulant or an impediment to the
creative process?*

N.M.: Literature can, of course, also be interpreted politically: this
is a narrowing, a reduction, that is not always justified. In the case
of literature with a clear political theme, it must also submit, if it
is literature, to the artistic criteria. In Romania we have for some
time been able to observe the rapid "institutionalization" of certain
books with a political theme—and the attempts of certain authors
to bypass strict literary standards. . . . The books in this category

---

[1] Lucian Blaga (1895–1961). Romanian poet, playwright, and philosophical essayist.

are frozen on a rigid pedestal of a hierarchy outside the literary domain (which they claim, nevertheless); they are protected from professional evaluation by critics, gradually becoming separated from the living reality of literature. Certain authors, by affixing themselves on a sort of prefabricated frieze of eminent figures, are quickly widening the distance between themselves and their colleagues whose merits are at least equal to their own, if not greater. The result is a disservice to literature in general and to writers preoccupied with political themes in particular, because suspicion is heightened and frustration is provoked. In a survey in the periodical *Amfiteatru* (*Amphitheater*), an author affirms, with reference to popular political novels, that "recently published books betray a sort of half-courage, i.e., *with permission from the police.*" This is a rather amazing turn of phrase, not because it has never been used before, but because it was written by an author who himself practiced at one time, to his considerable advantage, the theme of the hour. For the reader unable to verify the sources of an assertion like this, doubts about the publication of literary works—which until recently had been considered praiseworthy, if only for the liberating effect attributed to them—acquire unexpected impetus. We believe that political literature does not have more rights; rather, it has more obligations. These should entail an effort to bring things to the human level while aspiring to meet major aesthetic criteria, in order to realize a worthwhile achievement: an authentic testimony to true patriotism—a word that ought to be protected from trivialization, from frivolous demagogical manipulation. Good literature, of course, can be written on any subject. What I have just said can serve as an answer, perhaps indirectly, to the questions you have put to me. I could add that while political life can mobilize the creative resources of society, the artist is the first to feel it when political life becomes a force of fear, of restriction, of deviation of a nation's creative potential.

G.G.: *In general, how do you believe that a contemporary prose writer can participate in the public forum? How can he give his opinion on aspects of contemporary public life without ceasing to be a writer, that is, without projecting the concrete against the absolute?*

N.M.: No matter how complicated, circuitous, or labyrinthine the artist's creative sources and resources may be, and no matter what spectacular exceptions could be put before me, I believe that the writer must fulfill his artistic obligations in his work, be severe with himself and with his vocation; as a public person he must remain, no matter what the price, exigent with himself and with society, responsible, in the best sense of the word, to truth and to society; he must become the honest conscience in which his fellow man can believe. In its sublime attempt to capture the ineffable essence of man and the cosmos, literature invents its own laws, free of all authority outside its own standards for perfection. Artistic consciousness has to discover its echo, its validation, in a corresponding ethical consciousness. Let us not fool ourselves; it has never been easy to follow such a noble spiritual code.... The poverty, solitude, and lack of understanding that are a writer's lot seem at times easier to bear than the fact that he does not have access to the public forum, or that no one is interested in the opinion, good intentions, or potential competence that he embodies.

G.G.: *Might there be a significant rapport between irony and ethics? As someone who meditates on the theme of the buffoon, you do not ignore, I suppose, either the significance of the outraged figure of the poet behind his grotesque mask, or the disintegrating effects of this mask as an "abdication" from the ideal. In* Portrait de l'artiste en saltimbanque, *Jean Starobinski speaks of the game of irony as "a ridiculous epiphany of art and the artist," "a self-criticism directed against the aesthetic vocation itself." Doesn't this self-devouring of (at least) one of the categories of art trouble you?*

N.M.: This "self-devouring" troubles me profoundly, I admit; it seems to me to be one of the focal points of creative tension in all that I write. References to Starobinski are to be found, in any case, in my last book, whose title and theme contain—I would like to

point this out—an ironical substratum. . . .[2] The artist is not a
buffoon, even if he is seen as such by others, even if society forces
him to the distortion of makeup and farce. But given the pressures
of his environment—itself divided, distorted, flattened, twisted—
the ridiculous mask the artist wears is not a sign of acceptance, but
of rejection, even if this rejection is dissimulated and he is beginning
to prepare his revenge. The artist cannot "dignify" officialdom by
opposing it in a solemn fashion, because that would mean taking it
too seriously, and inadvertently reinforcing its authority, thus acknowledging that authority. He pushes the ridiculous to grotesque
proportions, but artistically, he creates, as you mentioned, a surfeit
of meanings.

"Classical" bourgeois society—impervious, opaque, bourgeois in
the Cartesian manner, mechanistic, Euclidian, we could call it—
erected a thick wall of obtuse opposition. The tragic, "unadapted"
hero tries to crack the soulless wall, but his thunderbolts ricochet
and hit the artist, still guilty of illusions, cutting down his fragile,
starlike, immortal silhouette. In today's frenetic, mixed-up society,
this chaos of consumerism and fear in which everything is scram-
bled and destroyed, the ridiculous runs the risk of "swallowing up"
art too. But the artist, even if he has been relegated to the position
of buffoon, tries to assume—even at the price of an apparent,
momentary abnegation of the self—an ambiguous stance, to place
himself on a shaky seesaw, to transform the loss into gain, the void
into expectation, into a sort of promise that hides the brilliance and
density of his "unseen face unmasked."

G.G.: *Do you believe in an unmasked artist, reduced to an irreducible nucleus, or is this a utopia that has no other purpose than to give
an aura to the fatal practice of dualism?*

N.M.: I can only repeat that I see no other reason for writing in
this life, so full of misery for some, greed for others, unless there

---

[2] The reference is to *Anii de ucenicie ai lui August Prostul* (*Auguste the Fool's Apprenticeship
Years*).

indeed exists an irreducible core in the artist's character, no matter how contradictory the masks in the "characters" he invents. Let us never confuse the sublime "game" of art with the backstage "games" of society. . . . In this tense end of the century, which has reached a summit of achievements and degradation, when from two opposite directions, money and lies, the weapons invented by man against man have acquired unimaginable destructive power, when mankind seems to be advancing, waveringly, along the edge of the abyss, toward the final conflict—giving "an aura to the fatal practice of dualism," as you say, would be the last (and final!) major failure of which we could accuse art. The "game" of art has never been anything more than fantasy, beauty, truth, intelligence, sanctity, smiles, shouts, and hope, the highest form of humanity, the joy of the spirit.

G.G.: *"Fair words make fools fain," says an English proverb. Do you think that the old "conflict" between fair words and authenticity can still impress an author who has been forewarned? What norms can a writer in all seriousness prescribe for himself in our time, when by virtue of modern poetics he is seen more likely as a "language operator" than as the hunter of a naked "authenticity" without regard to style?*

N.M.: I would never aspire to the title of "language operator." As for the hunter's occupation of laying traps and lying in wait, of gathering "proofs" of authenticity—in the manner, for example, of so-called documentary literature, which is more document than literature and interesting only as such—I do not believe that art exists outside creation. We can therefore speak of the authenticity of the *act* of creation and of the merits of a work. Are Proust and Joyce "operators" or "hunters"? Writing means words, the art of words. In art, truth does not exist outside its expression, as you precisely put it. Camil Petrescu,[3] who was no lover of "fair words," has a "style" that many could envy. . . . It is not beautiful words (or

[3] Camil Petrescu (1894–1957). Romanian novelist, poet, and philosopher.

ugly ones, for that matter), it is not stylistic achievements, to which any true writer enamored of his tools naturally aspires. The good writer is, of course, preoccupied with both authenticity and language—and he is repelled by the emptiness, the telltale falseness that clings to the ends of words. I do not doubt that great literature will be achieved through the coming together of language and authenticity, but also through divergences, or through countless unforeseeable ways, as it has always been achieved.

G.G.: *And now, if I may be "indiscreet": do you still collect humorous clippings from the contemporary press similar to those published in* Auguste the Fool's Apprenticeship Years, *in order to illustrate a bygone era? If, as I suspect, you answer yes, can you give me a couple of examples?*

N.M.: In *Auguste the Fool's Apprenticeship Years* I presented a fragmentary selection from one of the cultural periodicals from the period 1949–65 to suggest the atmosphere in which a young man—who is rather open, vaguely melancholic, probably intelligent, thirsting for culture, art, anything that might transcend the constraints of daily life—might have been able to shape or misshape his character. Only some of the citations were humorous; I wanted to show that that period, too, was alive and complex.

As for Auguste the Fool's *mature* years, there is clear evidence of continuity and, at the same time, there are marked differences from the previous period. There is now a pompous, deliberately celebratory aspect to those newspaper pages that at times takes on incredible proportions; there are, however, many more exact, realistic, and critical accounts about our daily lives. The price of conformism and the price of courage are much diminished today, while the guilt of those who commit themselves to twisting the truth and abusing language becomes obviously greater. . . . In order to remain consistent with our Auguste the Fool, we should limit ourselves to the cultural press. We could follow, for example, that clever young man with scissors who inserts weekly clippings of unintentional humor found in the press into the cultural pages in *Viaţa Studenţ-*

ească (*Student Life*). I do not have such clippings at hand, but we could instead recall a few other edifying examples, not at all innocent, that reflect a certain general condition. For a person who does not merely read but *lives* within a certain reality, the humorous aspect carries within it a serious core that should not be neglected. Perhaps it would serve some purpose for us to meditate on this. For some years, certain (what else can we call them?) "colleagues," specifically those who have been promoted by every loudspeaker and newspaper column of the popular media, authors who are not doing badly in terms of benefits and honors either, have been carrying on a sort of bitter, angry, "growling" campaign. In the end, they lend credence to a dubious portrait of the useless, immoral, unintelligible, confused, illiterate, demagogical, philistine, racketeering, vicious writer. The true writer—an albatross constantly wounded and always reopening its wings toward all and over all, toward the highest reaches of art—cannot and could never be described in this way.

In a Bucharest cultural journal that has acquired an unfortunate reputation as a result of its lack of polish and anticultural outbursts, a writer angered by the critics churned out, for months on end, a vehement, black series of articles against the most important of them. This writer published these articles in book form, not in Romania but in Italy, thus creating for himself an original, exclusive means for spreading (through slander) Romanian literature beyond our borders. In the same weekly, a still-young rhymester, recycled by a Herder fellowship, served up a warmed-over editorial, dreadful and chauvinistic, entitled—what else?—"Idealuri" ("Ideals"), the likes of which I did not believe we would ever again read in Romania. We need not go into its regrettable consequences here; suffice it to say that the young man, very eager to resuscitate a nostalgia for other times, was not fired and demoted, for the purpose of rest and therapy, to, let us say, a journal like *Albina* (*The Bee*) or *Sănătatea* (*Health*), but he is before television cameras and among the leading echelons of the press.

In a literary magazine supposed to be for young people (until it was decided to establish a *new order,* and an efficient new editorial board was installed in a matter of hours and kept in place for seven years—as in the Bible) a shameful page of invectives was published, on the death of Marin Preda,[4] about the writer's so-called infirmity and reduced capacities, and, if you please, his need for a drill sergeant of a nurse. There are many other examples, though it is hard to say how brutal or how ridiculous they are, if they are not both. In an influential journal a couple of months ago, a journalist—a university professor of literature, in fact—called, in language not at all exemplary, those with cultural opinions opposed to his (probably referring to his own colleagues on the faculty) "creatures without a homeland." We are reminded here of Mihai Ralea,[5] who once told of a dispute on a technical matter between two female physics students, in which the one left with no more arguments shouted at the other: "You're tubercular!"

The proliferation of certain aggressive acultural manifestations is not as worrying as the fact that there are no debates, even in the smaller literary magazines, with certain individuals who have journalistic immunity. What is there left to say about a known poet who, in so-called political verse, demands the abolition of a summer retreat for sculptors, or about an author who attacks "meritocracy" and the "supremacy of talent"? What are we to believe about the protective walls built up around certain books and authors, the "new" Tolstoy, the "new" Shakespeare, the "new" Mayakovsky, or the "new" Alexandru Toma?[6]

I believe that disagreements with those who maintain artificial tensions, petty, trivial intrigues, the hysterical and megalomaniacal small-town appetite for destruction and, in the end, self-destruction, should be more clearly expressed, at least in the literary press.

---

[4] Marin Preda (1922–1980). Arguably the greatest Romanian novelist of the postwar period. The reference is to Preda's excessive drinking.

[5] Mihai Ralea (1896–1964). Romanian essayist and sociologist, professor at the universities of Bucharest and Iași, and member of the Academy of Sciences.

[6] Alexandru Toma (1875–1954). Minor Romanian poet who after World War II devoted himself to "revolutionary" poetry.

"Confer value on the world if you wish to assert your own value," warned Goethe. I think that we can end on these words. With our thoughts on the minimum conditions necessary for normal intellectual endeavor, for the normal and free exercise of any profession, without which the creative impulse, as well as receptivity to and respect for values, is inconceivable.

ABOUT THE AUTHOR

Born in 1936, in Bukovina, Romania, Norman Manea was deported at the age of five to the Ukrainian internment camp of Transnistria. His fiction, which is preoccupied with the trauma of the Holocaust and with daily life in a totalitarian state, has been translated into more than ten languages. He is now a professor of literature at Bard College.